Fall Line

Carol Grant Sull

2008.

Carol Grant Sullivan

www.fallline.info

ISBN 0-9782282-0-0; 978-0-9782282-0-0

Production and Design Credits:

Publisher:	Penny A. Shore
Editor:	Jocelyn Laurence
Copy Editor:	Anna Miller
Cover Design:	Tudor Whiteley
	Eddie Chan
Photo Credits:	Grant family collection,
	UCC-Deborah Hickey,
	Andes-Kees

Every effort has been made to make this book as complete and accurate as possible, but no warranty or fitness is implied. The information is provided on an "as is" basis. The author and the publisher shall have neither liability nor responsibility to any person or entity with respect to any loss or damages arising from the information contained in this book.

SHORE
PUBLISHING

P. Shore & Associates Inc.
Shore Publishing Division
258 Adelaide Street East, Suite 302
Toronto, ON, M5A 1N1
416.923.6707
or send an email to pshore@shorepublishing.ca

Printed and bound in Canada.

This book is dedicated
To my parents, John Morgan Grant
and Mary Gertrude Newton Grant

To my husband, Brian Joseph Sullivan
and my children,
Hudson Alexander Grant Sullivan
and Hilary Stuart Grant Sullivan

Acknowledgements

ONE OF THE GREATEST GIFTS my parents gave me was their strength of love and family. I feel fortunate to have added my own love of nature and spirit of adventure to the mix.

It is the importance of these shared traits in my life that I believe pulled me through my recovery. As I tried to make sense of what happened that day on the mountain and what followed, I kept coming back to the importance of these key themes in my life.

This book is a true story of love, loss and survival. I must thank my husband Brian for his full support and encouragement. For it was Brian who kept a steady and watchful eye on me during the difficult times I had while writing this book. Without his love and devotion I may never have finished the story. His patience with me while I got my body and mind back to working order was unwavering. My children Hudson and Hilary have been an inspiration to me, and a steady reminder of how important life is to live fully. The power of their daily presence gave me the strength to return to a life of balance. I am eternally grateful to them. They too were deeply affected by all that happened.

Dr. Ruth Brooks, my family physician, made the suggestion that I write this story while examining me one day in her office at Women's College Hospital. Over a two-year span, Dr. Brooks guided me professionally through many specialist appointments and MRI scans to help me get to the bottom of my physical injuries and limitations.

I want to thank Judy Steed for agreeing to do this book with me. Her interest and commitment to me, my family and this story were unalterable. Her expertise in deepening the story and polishing it for market is without a doubt what makes her a pro. This book could not have been written without the assistance of Judy Steed.

Finally, our guide Kees, who was always supportive and willing to discuss and share his perspective of the accident. Thank you Kees for your friendship, compassion and leadership both on and off the mountain.

During the early days after the accident I felt very alone with my injuries and overwhelmed by my condition and my sense of responsibility for what happened.

I owe so much to the names mentioned here because of the help and support they gave me in writing this book and ultimately getting me back to the mountains.

There is little doubt that I was born under a lucky star.

Table of Contents

Prologue   The Fall   13

Chapter 1   Getting Ready   15

Chapter 2   The North   21

Chapter 3   Death & Loss   29

Chapter 4   Paradise Found   37

Chapter 5   Struggle for Balance   51

Chapter 6   The Turning Point   77

Chapter 7   The Accident   87

Chapter 8   Recovery & Rehab   105

Chapter 9   From Nightmares to Dreams   131

Glossary   Useful Terms   145

ROUTE OF THE EXPEDITION AND FALL

A. First rest stop
B. Midway point
C. Final rehydration before ascent to summit
D. The summit
E. Entry point to the couloir
F. Start of fall
G. End of fall

Start of
Climb

E

F

Start of
Expedition

PROLOGUE

The Fall

August 11, 2004

IT IS A BLUEBIRD DAY, as they say in the mountains, not a cloud in the sky. The freedom to fly—that's what we're chasing today in Las Leñas, laying down our own high speed tracks, deep in fresh powder, high atop the Andes Mountains in the Mendoza province of Argentina. The second largest chain of mountains in the world, the Andes are raw, treacherous and known for the best off-piste (out of bounds) skiing—my kind of skiing.

I am with Brian, my husband, whom I love more than life itself, celebrating our 21st wedding anniversary. We are seasoned high altitude skiers accompanied by our trusted guide Kees, returning to Las Leñas for the second time. I am anticipating a phenomenal, repeat performance of last year, when we had climbed every day and enjoyed steep verticals that fell for 3,000 to 4,000 feet with epic powder everywhere. We thought the skiing beat anything extreme we had experienced in Chamonix, Argentierre, Whistler, St. Anton,

Vail, Jackson Hole, Verbier, Engleberg, Alagna, the Monashees, Purcells and Bugaboos included. It is an exhausting climb up to the summit, and we celebrate our triumph at close to 14,000 feet in elevation. We're on top of the world. We rest a few minutes to drink in the beauty of our surroundings, the rugged, snow-capped peaks of the Andes towering around us. As we begin to search for the best opening (to ski down), the steepness takes my breath away. I am feeling apprehensive. This is a no-fall zone.

Brian shoves off the cornice and disappears from view. I wait until he radios up, then I push off. It's a wild vertical, icy and unforgiving. Six turns into the chute, I can't hold on, I've lost my balance, I am in space, back diving, eyes wide open, staring backwards down the narrow chute. I am airborne. I have fallen off the mountain.

They say that in the moment before death, your life flashes before your eyes. Not for me. My body is taken over by a fierce primal instinct: the survival instinct. It grabs me with a power that would be frightening if it wasn't such a familiar ally. It was born into me, infused into every cell of my being, in the North.

In a distant patrol hut, a mountain patroller scans the high hazard area through a telescope. He sees a body hurtling off "The Blade," the steepest chute on Cerro Torrecillas. He assumes he's witnessed a death on the mountain.

CHAPTER ONE

Getting Ready
A Special Mission

June 28 – July 31, 2004

I LEFT MY HOUSE IN TORONTO and flew to Vancouver with my nine-year-old daughter, Hilary. We grabbed our bags off the carousel and went to the long-term parking lot, where we found the old gray mare, a 1989 silver Volvo that had once belonged to my dear mother-in-law. We buckled our seat belts, smiled at each other in anticipation of the excitement that was to come, and headed up the Sea to Sky Highway to my favourite place, Blueberry Hill, overlooking the town of Whistler. It was a two-hour drive along the Pacific Ocean, up into the Coast Mountains—one of the most scenic highways in North America—and even after 25 years I had never tired of the views. When I finally got out of the car, standing in the driveway at Blueberry Hill, I soaked up the incredible sight of the mountains rising up all around us. I felt so lucky to be there, so relieved to be out of the Toronto rat race. I was home.

Over the years since Brian and I had started coming to Whistler, winter and summer, the village had changed from a sleepy little haven for hard core skiing fanatics to a mecca for jet-setters and dot-commers. Now a sophisticated, world class ski resort, scheduled to host the 2010 Winter Olympic Games, Whistler was full of trendy restaurants and hip boutiques, which I'd enjoyed in the past. But this summer was going to be different. I was on a special mission: to train for an 18-day trip to the Andes. I was pumped. I would get to hang out with Hilary for a whole month; we'd cycle on mountain paths to Rainbow Lake and Lost Lake and go swimming, and pick berries in the Pemberton Valley—luscious strawberries and raspberries for pies and jams like my mother used to make up North. I wasn't much of a cook, but the berries in the Pemberton Valley inspired me. And while Hilary was enrolled in skiing and tennis camps, I would work out.

I was on the final stretch of an eight-month leave of absence from my job as a marketing consultant to Visa Canada. I had spent the previous six months tagging along behind my son, Hudson, who was in his final year of high school and would soon be leaving home to go to university. The prospect of losing him had somewhat unhinged me. I had such an elevated awareness about his departure that I was counting down the days with trepidation. It was a very emotional time for me. I wanted to be with him as much as I possibly could. "You're smothering me, not mothering me," Hudson would joke as I kept offering to drive him to school or pick him up. (He had his own car.) The family thought my behaviour was out of character and hysterically funny. I was serious about it. I didn't tell them why I was doing it. I didn't fully understand it myself.

Hudson was going to turn 18 on July 12. To mark his graduation, Brian and I had decided to take him to Portillo,

Chile, the most secluded, breathtaking ski resort in South America. It was like the most exquisite hotel in St. Moritz—except it was tucked away into a remote part of the Andes. This was the ultimate skiing destination, the greatest gift, the most memorable experience we could think of, to recognize Hudson's passage to maturity. For us, this was a natural choice. Families have things they do together, interests they share. The Sullivans ski. We were addicted to extreme skiing. Hudson had been skiing with us since he was two years old, hiking and climbing in the backcountry since he was seven, traveling with us all over the world in our search for the most exotic mountain areas, the deepest snow, the thrill of pushing ourselves to the edge. Now he was all grown up and ready to launch himself into the world, a strong, intelligent, confident young man. Celebrating the occasion was hugely important to me—I treasure family rituals—and this would help me face the fact that he was leaving home. He was on my mind constantly. I was strangely concerned about his well-being and haunted by my own past. When I was his age, my father died. The sense of loss had never left me, but now it was rising up again, filling me with the old loneliness, the aching emptiness.

I hoped our trip to Portillo would break the spell, free me from the sadness that seemed to have been triggered by Hudson's imminent departure. I couldn't wait to ski the extreme, the powder, the steeps and most exciting of all, the gorgeous Andes Mountains of Chile and Argentina. Best for skiing in July and August—the South American winter occurring during the North American summer—the Andes attract international skiers seeking the steep vertical terrain and the seduction of the snow, up to 770 cm thick. Brian and I had skied in thigh-deep powder on our first trip to the Andes the year before, to celebrate our 20th wedding anniversary, and we'd loved the climbs, the sun and the challenge of vertigo. And the night life, I have to confess. (Before I'd left for the trip, I'd been luxuriating in a La Prairie facial at Holt Renfrew when one of the La Prairie executives had appeared from the New York office. I'd told her I was going to Argentina to ski. Turned out she had been a ski racer and had spent her summers training in Las Leñas. "What's the night life like?" I'd asked, thinking *fleecies, jeans, long underwear.* She'd clued me in. "It's really fancy, really hot, a flashy, sexy scene. Take your best stuff. Everybody gets dressed up for the disco and the casino.")

We had a plan: Hudson would spend ten days with us in the Chilean Andes, with our guide, and then fly home alone to pack for his first year studies at Notre Dame. Brian and I would proceed with the guide to Las Leñas for an extra week. Then we'd return to Toronto, Hilary would be back from summer camp, and we'd all drive Hudson to university for his orientation.

The itinerary was set, the bookings were made, all I had to do was complete a fierce training schedule to ensure I would be at the elite performance level necessary for the Andes. Which is why I'd taken off for Whistler, where I could better concentrate on my physical regimen, far from the smog and pressures of my Toronto life. While little Hilary went off to ski camp on the Blackcomb Glacier at 7:30 in the morning—it's too hot to summer ski on the glacier in the afternoon; the sun melts the snow—I ran up and down the mountain for 30 to 45 minutes, to improve my cardio endurance. Skiing in the high altitude of the Andes requires grueling preparation but I was up for it. I had never felt so motivated in my life, but I wasn't sure why. Something was happening inside me, and it had to do with Hudson.

As I pounded up and down, I thought about my son. Had I done enough for him? Had I given him the support and guidance he needed? Would he be ready to live on his own? In the gym at the Whistler Tennis Club in the afternoon, while Hilary played tennis, I worked out with my west-coast trainer. I carried 20 pound weights in each hand and did sets of 30 squats and lunges and 60 sets of step-ups on a bench, up and down, again and again, building up my quads. I was determined to be strong enough to keep up with the boys—Brian and Hudson—in the backcountry.

My trainer was big on stretches—hamstrings, glutes, lower back, quads, inner thighs, outer thighs, pecs, triceps and calves. The stretching alone took 40 minutes. The workouts were strenuous and went on for two hours. When I wasn't at the gym, I carried on at home, on my own, every day. Working out so hard physically released a lot of emotion in me; sometimes I found myself crying when I ran. It was a natural progression from thinking about Hudson and this major transition in his life to my own experience at the same age. It had been the worst time of my life.

I'd lost my father, my sense of family and the paradise in which I'd been raised. And I'd left the North, never to live there again. For a young woman whose upbringing had been framed by powerful forces—love of nature and love of family, set in a context of unrelenting competition and risk taking—it was like losing everything, all at once.

CHAPTER TWO

The North

1957–1975

MY CHILDHOOD WAS SET, my character shaped, in a vast landscape of extraordinary power: the wilderness, lakes and rivers, trees and wildlife of Northern Ontario. In summer, endless green forests and sparkling blue water. In winter, rolling hills blanketed with fresh snow, glistening white. The silence, the peace, the harmony of nature, the brilliance of stars in an inky black sky.

I was born in 1957 into a large, boisterous Irish-Scots family, the ninth of eleven children and the third and last daughter. We lived in a big red brick house that had once belonged to my maternal grandparents in "downtown" New Liskeard, at the corner of Whitewood and John. I'm not sure if New Liskeard, population 5,000, on the shores of Lake Temiskaming, halfway between Lake Ontario and James Bay—as the crow flies—can be said to have a downtown. But for me, it was the center of the universe. We had a rink in the backyard where we skated and played hockey for hours every day, and a sense of growing up in the great outdoors, in a limitless space that enabled us to explore, take risks and think big. We swam, canoed, rode horses, played sports. We were never confined. The front door was never locked.

At the St. Bernard Ski Club, a short drive out of town, we made fun of the "chalet skiers" who hung out drinking hot chocolate all day because of the cold. Heaven forbid if Dad caught one of us inside, being "a chalet skier." My father was an intensely competitive taskmaster. He expected his children to strive to be the best. Performance was critical. There was zero tolerance for failure. We were groomed to be highly ambitious, avoid mistakes, never back down. *What, you didn't do it? What happened? Try again.* We were taught to be daring and bold. We were risk takers, but not reckless fools.

In summer, we'd hike through the woods to the fire tower, to pick blueberries. The tower, used by forest rangers to watch for fires, was built high up, above the tree tops. It was huge, viewed through the eyes of a child. And every summer, it was a rite of passage for us to climb that tower. If the older boys climbed it when they were six, you had to climb it when you were six. No matter how scared you were, you had to do it. If Peter got up on one water ski when he was seven, you had to try to do it too. Everything was about effort. Our parents pushed us to excel and we internalized their expectations without realizing it. They were doing what came naturally to them.

My father, John Morgan Grant, was descended from Scottish Highlanders who'd settled in North America, in the state of New York, in the early 1700s and migrated to Canada as United Empire Loyalists in 1784. His Gaelic-speaking father, Peter Grant, had lost his right arm in a sawmill accident at 18 and lived until 82 using an artificial arm made from steel and rawhide, hinged at the elbow, with a hook on the end. He established the P.J. Grant Lumber Co. in New Liskeard in the early 1900s and became a legendary character in the North. His sawmill cut eight million board feet a season and exported most of its lumber to Great Britain. He was the mayor of New Liskeard and a frequent recipient of awards from the Lumbermen's Safety Association.

When Morgan Grant met Gertrude Newton—an ardent figure skater—at the local rink, they were teenagers, sent away to boarding schools every fall, both determined to come back and live in the North. Gertie was a strong-willed Irish Catholic girl, educated by nuns. The Grants were strict Presbyterians, ruled by an intense work ethic. When Morgan and Gertie got married in 1943, he was agreeable to her raising the children Catholic. While Gertie devoted herself to her expanding family, Morgan was busy expanding his father's lumber business, eventually creating an empire that included construction, road building, farming, and transportation. He worked like a Trojan; he was intensely driven and ambitious. The only peaceful time of the week for him was Sunday morning, seeing his wife and eleven children off to Mass, while he headed out to his fields. He owned 1,000 acres of farmland and loved animals; caring for his cattle and horses was his hobby.

Everybody knew my father. An indomitable character, he was larger than life, hugely energetic and intimidating in certain situations. Devoted to his family, he loved his wife deeply and was known for being highly-principled and indefatigable—which made his early death so shocking, so tragic.

Maybe because I was the last girl, I felt very close to Dad. Maybe he wanted me to feel special because of my eye problem. I had a wandering eye (strabismus) brought on, Mom thought, by a fever when I was 4 years old. Between the ages of 4 and 19, I had five operations to correct the eye at the Hospital for Sick Children in Toronto. I was very, very scared of the surgery and of being put "out" under anesthetic, but my mother was always there when I woke up. She went to a lot of trouble to get the doctors to explain the procedures (they actually took the eye out of the socket during surgery) and to make sure my eye opened and was bathed properly. I still have a lot of scar tissue from those operations, which left me with the ability to only see out of one eye at a time. I'm an "alternator." The eyes don't "fuse." I have poor peripheral vision and limited depth perception, but I learned to compensate by switching from one eye to the other. It's the equivalent, I guess, of covering one eye with a patch, then rapidly switching sides. As a child, I was never made to feel "odd" or "different," though I probably got a little extra attention from my parents because of all the surgeries. I played all the sports, joined all the teams and my parents made sure I was "one of the gang."

Family life was full of tomfoolery and horseplay, but Mom worked hard to keep order. She instilled a strong sense of discipline in all of us. Dinner was served at 6 pm sharp every evening, and as the clock ticked closer to the hour—and the girls set the table on a fresh white linen tablecloth—we'd watch for Dad's Oldsmobile to turn into the driveway. (We were a General Motors family. No Fords for us!) Only then did we troop to the table and take our seats—the same places every night. The food was plentiful and the conversation bursting with athletic dares and stories of the latest conquests at school, work and on the sports field. There was no end to the frightening tales of riding accidents, water ski shows, jumping trials, racing car escapades, hockey showdowns, go-cart crashes, figure skating carnivals and football games. With 11 children ranging in age over 17 years, and eight of the most competitive boys to ever surface in one family, what choice did I have but to keep up?

Mom held her own—with lots of household help—and even provided a touch of glamour. Every Friday afternoon from 2 to 4 pm, she had her hair and nails done at the local salon (the only time she had to herself). The fresh hairdo was supposed to last the week, but usually lost its shape within hours of coming back home. She wasn't fussed. She moved through the mayhem—children wrestling and chasing each other up and down stairs—in heels, hose and beautifully tailored dresses. She taught me an important lesson about staying attractive to my husband. It was a big thrill to accompany her on a shopping trip to Toronto, where she sipped tea while she was shown the designer collections at Holt Renfrew and Creeds. I browsed through the racks and was especially excited when we attended private fashion shows with models showing off the latest designs. I took pride in knowing Mom's favourite labels: Yves St. Laurent, Ungaro and Chanel.

My eldest sister, Susan, who was like a surrogate mother to me, growing up, says I idealized family life, that it was rush, rush, rush, Mom scolding 11 children to get us dressed, get us going, hurry up, do this, don't do that, stop fighting—but I don't remember it that way. Susan had to help Mom, as a senior member of the family. I was always outdoors playing. I never did learn (or like) to cook, clean or sew.

We spent our summers at Twin Lakes, at the cottage—a magnificent old log house with pine floors, a stone fireplace and a big sailing ship on the mantelpiece that was loaded with red ribbons from the annual Twin Lakes Regatta going back to the 1950s. There were stone breakwater-walls along the shoreline, a tall diving tower at the end of the dock, and two separate cabins, one for the boys and one for the girls. And stables where Dad brought the horses for the summer. We'd swim and water-ski, go horseback riding, explore the woods, sit around bonfires at night and watch the Northern Lights flash across the sky—rose colours, purples, pinks, and whites undulating in all their mesmerizing glory. It was a magical place, a madhouse all summer long. Mom and Susan spent hours driving the boats, dragging us around the lake on water skis, ensuring each of us had a chance. My older brothers would be airborne: one would buzz the cottage with his seaplane, another would zip around in his helicopter and a third would fly through the air, kite-skiing. It was a wildly exciting place to grow up.

I was a good student and a decent figure skater. Walking to the rink in pre-dawn darkness at 40 degrees below zero, listening to the sound of snow crunching under my boots, I dreamed of becoming a professional figure skater, touring with the Ice Capades. I skated seven days a week, on the ice at 6 am for lessons three times a week, skating until 8:20 am, back at the rink after school most days. Sometimes my father would surprise me and drop by the arena at the very last moment of my lesson. If I wasn't on the ice, he'd look at me sternly. "I came to see you skate," he'd say. "You weren't skating. I'm paying for your lessons and you don't get off early." The message was clear: Stay until the last moment, work until the last second, never slack off.

There was never any doubt about Dad's own effort or commitment. We always had a sense of his enormous capacity, mentally and physically, to deal with his vast range of business interests, coping with the sheer geographical reach of his work, the land, its resources, the highways, the wilderness. My brothers were expected to work in the business during their teenage years and they were pushed hard—up at 5 am to plow highways during a blizzard if Dad was short of staff. He was often going off to visit logging camps in Matachewan and lumber operations in Elk Lake. In summer the boys went with him. He was tough, like his own father, and hard on the boys— for their own good, as he saw it.

Not as much was expected of the girls because we weren't going to take over the family business. But I didn't quite get the message. I didn't see the difference between the girls and the boys, and tried to live up to Dad's high expectations. I didn't know why I couldn't be set up to be as successful as the boys. In fact, I thought I should.

Certainly Dad set the bar high. He worked tirelessly to ensure that the economic development of the North was sustained and that critical services such as the local health care system were protected. He fought hard for what he believed in and expected us, his children, to carry his legacy forward, to contribute to the community and excel in all our endeavours. I felt a special sense of being protected and guided by Dad. My world was rock solid, I thought. Everything was as it should be. Then, suddenly, he got sick. I had no way of knowing how quickly his life would come to an end and with it, my family's tight-knit cohesion.

CHAPTER THREE

Death & Loss

1973-1980

IN 1973, I WAS 16 YEARS OLD, a good student, an accomplished figure skater and a keen competitive skier. Skating seven days a week plus skiing on the weekends, I was training as if I were going to become a professional athlete—not surprising in a family of children who excelled at sports. But I was at a crossroads in my life. I'd watched my hockey-mad older brothers—a couple of them so good they'd been scouted by the National Hockey League—redirect their energies and make plans for "The Future," with Dad's guidance. The Future seemed to be a complicated place requiring a great deal of discussion. For my older brothers, it meant going to university and applying themselves in areas that would be useful to the family business—engineering, business and management studies. There was a heightened sense of purpose and "destiny" surrounding my brothers, given the importance of their role in taking the business into The Future, which was all wrapped up with Dad and three generations of Grants who'd built a tightly controlled group of companies that were privately owned. Their hardships, vision and work ethic had been transmuted into a legacy that would be carried on by my brothers. It was an awesome responsibility—and I wanted to be part of it but I didn't know how. I counted on my father to guide me, as he had the others, when I got older.

One of my favourite times with Dad was when he'd get up early and drive me to the arena for my morning skating lesson. It was a rare treat to stay warm in his car instead of trudging through dark deserted streets in the freezing cold at 6 a.m. (So cold that Mom made me cover my face to prevent frostbite; when I was 14 years old, she had me wearing a heavy raccoon coat to keep warm on those walks.)

One morning when Dad was driving me, I sat beside him on the front seat, still groggy from sleep, and told him about the extraordinary nightmare I was trying to shake off. I'd dreamed I was in a huge stadium. I was holding a bag of popcorn, watching an exciting baseball game, utterly enthralled, when suddenly the whole stadium blew up. It was a massive explosion. My popcorn was swirling all around me when I woke up, drenched in sweat, terrified. It felt like the end of the world. I shuddered in horror.

I looked at my father and was reassured by his presence. Yet I couldn't shake the looming sense of doom. Was it a premonition? Did I sense that he was sick? That his death, only a few years away, would be like a stadium explosion in which everything was destroyed?

As I matured, I picked up signals from my parents that they didn't approve of me wanting to join the Ice Capades. I began to wonder what else might be out there for me. I admired my mother but her life was rather narrow, I thought. I didn't want to have eleven children and couldn't imagine devoting myself to a huge family the way she did. She loved her life but she was on the sidelines in the business arena in which Dad dominated. He was the visionary, the financier, the boss.

Reading newspapers and watching TV, I saw that women were reaching into the business world and experimenting with meaningful work outside their homes. This I found very interesting. My older sister had trained to be a nurse. What would I be? I felt an urgent need to find an exciting career. I thought perhaps law. What did lawyers really do? Make decisions, go to court, gain justice for those deserving. This was appealing, yet I'd done well in the sciences and could have gone into a medical field. I was confused and needed direction. I wanted to contribute to the family and somehow set myself apart from my older, high-achieving brothers and sisters. But I didn't need to worry, I told myself, Dad would help me. He had the right answer for everything.

Then, all of a sudden, the rhythm and routine of our lives was shattered. Out of the blue, my father—who never got sick, who was always ready for any crisis—was diagnosed with colon cancer and taken away to hospital. It wasn't just like having the rug pulled out from under me, it was like a gaping chasm opened beneath my feet. I was left at home with two younger brothers and stern old Mrs. Tessier, our housekeeper. I watched helplessly as my parents disappeared from my life. Mom spent most of her time with Dad at Toronto General Hospital, where she was consumed by his condition, trying to orchestrate cancer specialists to find a cure. The drive to Toronto took more than six hours and she didn't come home very often. When she did, she sometimes had Dad in the back of her station wagon, seats laid flat with a mattress on top so he could rest during the long drive. He was desperate to get home, to see his family and check in with his business, but he was so weak he could barely function. He'd lie in bed, recuperating from the trip, and then have to turn around and have Mom drive him back to the hospital.

What had been a very happy childhood fast became a miserable last few teenage years for me. The sense of belonging to an enormous, loving, fiercely competitive, boisterous family got lost as we all spiraled downward at signs of Dad's failing health. I didn't realize how severe the situation was, at first, and found the whole obsession with his condition tiresome. Dad had never been sick; he would get better—any other outcome was unthinkable. However, Mom could think of nothing and no one but him, and he seemed to have forgotten all about me—right when I needed him the most.

At the age of 17, I decided to take matters into my own hands. I got a ride to Toronto, made my way to the hospital and wandered through the maze of corridors until I found my father's room. I planned out what I would say, and how he would listen, assess my situation and show me the way. Almost trembling with the pent-up need to get his advice—I'd heard him talk to my older brothers about what to study, what careers to pursue, how to make the best contributions to the family business—I sat down at his bedside, anticipating great words of wisdom. I imagined he'd been lying there thinking about me for weeks, since he had nothing else to do.

I took a deep breath, ready to launch into my speech, and looked at my father. He was pale and breathing lightly. He looked weak and frail. I held his hand. His eyelids fluttered. "Dad, it's time for me to choose the courses I should take at university. I start applying soon. I'll be leaving home next fall. My marks are excellent and I can do anything I want. What do you think I would be good at? I need to know from you now."

His eyes opened but they were flat, lifeless. There was a long pause. When he spoke, his voice was faint. "I don't know," he said, and his eyes closed. I waited, but there was nothing more. Those were the last words he ever spoke to me. I left the hospital in shock that cold, dreary winter afternoon, disappointed and angry. I felt cheated, robbed. Feelings of despair stuck with me for a long, long time. There was no guidance or counsel for me. I was the little one and my father had run out of time. Soon afterward he died at the age of 55. His death changed my life forever. The sense of loss was enormous, inexplicable. *I will never be the same again*, I thought, *I will have to push on alone*. To this day, I believe that when a child loses a parent, it is life altering. The sadness is always with me.

It was a harsh winter. The coldness outside matched the chill in my heart. My father's body lay in the living room at home for three days as hundreds of people filed into the house to pay their respects. I was in grade 13, my last year of high school, but I stayed at home for the week to help Mom and the rest of the family cope with all the people. "He was so young," they said. "I can't believe he's gone." They talked about what a life force he had been, what good things he had done for the community, for the entire North. The Grants lived long, full lives. This was not in the script. But Dad was dead. I was numb. The funeral was unbearable. The pallbearers were loyal employees from the mill, men who'd known Dad forever. Everyone looked grief-stricken. Mom was in shock.

Nothing changed and everything changed. The Grants are stoic. Keep a stiff upper lip and don't show weakness. There were no tears, no long mourning period. The house looked the same but Dad wasn't there to direct, guide, provide the strength. It was like having the rudder yanked off the bottom of a boat, and waiting for the boat to find its balance and get back on course. The days went by and I kept thinking he'd appear at six o'clock, to resume his normal schedule. I'd watch for his Oldsmobile to turn up the driveway, but it never came. My older brothers were already set up, on their own, running the business, and it continued to thrive, as he had planned. They had children and wives to look after. My younger brothers played hockey. Life went on. I went into a void.

Dad's personal photos, books, letters and belongings were bundled up and taken away. I don't know where they went, but over time they disappeared. I was left with only two family photographs of him in my possession.

Mother was never really herself again. She'd lost the center of her universe. She moved to an apartment in Toronto (which I shared with her when I came to the city), she visited her grown children and their families, and kept the house in New Liskeard and the cottage. Though she lived another 20 years, she was absent in her grief and increasingly preoccupied with health problems. Slowly, she faded away.

I was confused and lost. But that summer, the summer of 1976, before I left home to go to university, Brian Sullivan came into my life at the cottage during the Twin Lakes Regatta. I was in charge of organizing the diving, swimming, sailing, canoe and lawn races for the families on the lake. With eleven competitive children, the Grants had always been a major force at the regatta, competing in all the races, eager to take home red ribbons and trophies, to delight our parents.

Brian was 19 years old, a year older than me, and already at university, which impressed me. He came up to the lake every summer and I'd seen him around before but this was the first time we'd really connected. His mother and grandmother had cottages on the lake—they were well known in the area. But Brian had grown up in Toronto, where his father, Glenn Alexander Sullivan, was a respected lawyer. Brian was very athletic, like his dad, and fresh from the 1976 Montreal Olympics, where he was on Canada's national race committee for sailing. He was full of stories about the excitement of the Olympics and he was a lot of fun to be around. Despite the fog of grief I was in, I noticed him. He asked me to save a dance for him at the pavilion that night, and I did. There was an instant attraction. He wasn't intimidated by the competitive force of my family. In fact, he enjoyed it. My brothers were "tough guys, not like city boys," he told me later, with admiration. As Brian saw it, my father had promoted a positive sense of competition among his boys. "Thought it would be good for them and good for the business. He was right."

I didn't know it at the time, but Brian's father had died of leukemia a few years earlier, when Brian was only 15. Our mutual loss would become a deep bond between us. We were both fatherless. Brian seemed to handle his father's death quite well, guided by his mother, Helen, who was his father's second wife. Helen had been Glenn Sullivan's legal secretary, marrying him after the death of his first wife. Glenn was 25 years older than Helen, which meant that when Brian was born, his father was in his late 50s. Thus Brian grew up with an older father who was in his 70s when he died. "I knew when I married your dad that he wouldn't outlive me," Helen told Brian. She went back to work (for an obstetrician) and resumed her life. So did Brian. There was nothing holding him back. And as I would learn, he was every bit as competitive as my brothers.

That fall, I left the town I loved to go to the University of Western Ontario, in London. I left everything behind: my family, my place in the world, the lakes and rivers and forests that were the paradise of my childhood. I descended into bleak terrain. My father was gone, my mother was grieving and I was adrift. It was expected that I would excel at university, and I went through the motions of being a good student, but I didn't flourish. I'd lost the academic curiosity that I'd had in high school; no one in the family noticed. Joining the women's fraternity Kappa Alpha Theta was the most grounding experience I had. I lived at the Theta house, sat on the executive committee, became treasurer, hired the cook and paid the bills. I had friends but I was unfocused intellectually, bouncing from political science to economics and business. I got a solid degree but my heart wasn't in it. Those were lost years. One of the bright spots was when Brian and I would connect to go skiing. He was my link to the joy I had known in the North. I dated other guys but I did not discover the passion that would animate my adult life until I travelled to the Rocky Mountains.

CHAPTER FOUR

Paradise Found

The Rocky Mountains

1980-1986

IN 1980 I GRADUATED from university and moved west, to Banff, Alberta. I'd spent the three previous summers there, mainly at the Banff Springs Hotel, working as a tour guide in the Canadian Rocky Mountains. As a student, I took tourists, mostly American and British, on sightseeing trips to the Valley of the Ten Peaks, Lake Louise, the Columbia Icefield and Jasper. The first time I had seen these places—when I was a teenager and my parents took me to the Rockies—I couldn't believe I lived in a country with such astounding natural beauty. It was surreal in its impact.

Now, in my first full-time job, I was working for the Lake Louise Ski Area, then the largest ski area in Canada and one of the most beautiful in the world. Tucked into Banff National Park, it offers majestic skiing and climbing for adventurers who thirst for challenging terrain and magnificent views. It was here, with Brian Sullivan, that my spirit was reborn. Looking back, I realize that I was recreating the life I had had in the

North, a simple athletic life lived mainly outdoors—with the addition of incredible mountains.

The job at Lake Louise was almost too good to be true—I was so young to have such a peak experience, and it came with a lifestyle in perfect sync with my instincts, interests and strengths. I was skiing or hiking on the mountains every spare moment I had, and at work I was learning the business of operating one of the great natural wonders of the world. My desk was in the cavernous lobby of the Banff Springs Hotel, an iconic resort built by Canadian Pacific Railway in 1888 in the style of a Scottish castle. Close to the hot springs for which the hotel was named, it has a view to die for: overlooking the sweeping Bow Valley toward the grandeur of Mount Rundle.

My working hours were 7 to 9 in the morning, and 5 to 8 in the evening. In between, I skied solidly every day from November to May. My task was to devise marketing and advertising campaigns to reach consumers locally and internationally, including Olympic skiers such as Ken Read and Kerrin Lee-Gartner who had ties to Lake Louise. My family back east thought I was on vacation. The Grants are resource-based entrepreneurs and couldn't imagine that skiing was a serious business. They thought I was a ski bum. Which I guess I was, in a way.

I blossomed into a happy young woman. I dated celebrities and politicians who visited the area, including former Prime Minister Pierre Trudeau. These were never serious pursuits but simply just for fun. I was learning vital lessons in business and had valuable mentors. Sir Rodney Touche gave me my first big break. The head of the holding company that owned the Lake Louise Ski Area, Rodney was a sophisticated businessman who loved skiing and adored the

Rockies. After I'd worked at Lake Louise for only a year, he took a chance on me and offered me the job of director of marketing. I was 24 years old, managing an advertising budget that exceeded $1 million—a rare opportunity for someone of my limited experience in the early 1980s. I worked hard for Rodney. I wrote my first integrated marketing plan, dividing the budget among all the pieces of the mix: TV, radio, print media, public relations, and direct sales. I contacted radio and TV stations and personally negotiated with media sales reps to get the best deal for Lake Louise. Because we didn't have a large staff, I learned the business from the ground up. It was great training. And we accomplished some very exciting firsts at Lake Louise—the first-ever discount skiing card, destination hotel packages and, in the early 1980's, we opened up the Lake Louise hotels for winter ski guests.

My dream of making something of myself was coming together. I was pushing the envelope as a young woman in management, as the only female on the management committee and easily 20 years younger than my male colleagues. I was so keen on ascending the corporate ladder that I moved to Calgary for two winters to work 9-5, Monday to Friday, out of the city office—which reduced my skiing time considerably. But it was worth it. The sport and business of skiing, especially in the mountains of North America, was surging in consumer and investor interest. I was at the epicentre of a dynamic industry, doing something I loved. And I was living in the mountains. Ultimately I became a risk taker in business and in skiing as a direct result of my early experiences in the Canadian Rockies. This was the birthplace of my extreme skiing adventures. I was hooked on the power of the mountains to move me like nothing else had ever done.

I was falling in love—with the mountains, and with Brian. He was living and working in Calgary and would drive up to Banff on weekends to ski with me. We bonded in nature, in our love of the great outdoors and our passion for the challenges and risks of off-piste skiing. We abandoned the tame terrain of groomed hills served by up-and-down chair lifts, and sought out long climbs in remote wilderness terrain, skiing through fluffy white powder that no one else had touched. I saw moose and bears coming out of the woods, deer and elk roaming the shorelines. I found a paradise to replace the one I'd lost—and a partner to share it with.

We learned to ski off piste simply by doing it. Brian took the lead, at first. We'd get up early and go, just the two of us, exploring, learning, falling, picking ourselves up and trying again. In the early 1980s we hardly ever ran into any other women. Men thought women were liabilities in the backcountry, Brian told me. "Men are afraid women will crack up and the guys will have to carry them out." He said I was different. "What do you expect?" I said. "I grew up in the North with ten brothers and sisters."

Before heading out on the mountain, we'd talk to pro patrollers and trail crew about where to go, where it was safe, what areas were closed due to snowfall accumulation and where there was no risk of an avalanche. We read up on snow safety and understood the sheer strength and danger of snow. We learned to watch for fracture lines—cracks in the snow— that were sometimes visible when we crossed open terrain; cracks were the first sign of a potential avalanche. We watched for places where the snow loaded up, where the wrong move could bring snow crashing down on top of us. Such a paradox: that something so soft, that starts out as crystals in clouds, can become so powerful, so deadly. Brian saw things, early on, that scared him, though he didn't tell me he was scared until years later. A couple of guys we knew got buried by an avalanche—the whole slope came down on top of them, just outside Lake Louise—but they got out. Brian saw an avalanche knock down large trees, snapping the trunks like twigs.

In the European Alps, about 120 people are killed every year by snow falling in the form of avalanches. In the U.S., the annual death toll is 14, in Canada, 7—one of them, sadly, Michel Trudeau, the son of Pierre Trudeau. It can happen in the blink of an eye. Brian had been in a few surface slides, with snow falling down behind him, but he was lucky enough to get out. It didn't happen to me, but I've heard the sound of an avalanche, a roar like the rumble of thunder but much heavier, like an earthquake—it shakes you to the core. That's why there are warnings everywhere. Often when you ski into the backcountry, you pass signs that say, "Beyond this point, you're on your own. If you need to be rescued, it will be at your full cost." At various ski areas around the world, we have had to sign insurance releases acknowledging that the ski resort was not responsible for us.

Snow could be heavy or hard-packed, icy or granular; we liked it light and fluffy. We loved the long runs in virgin powder. Backcountry skiing in powder looks effortless but it can be exhausting and dangerous, going through snow that is waist-deep. It is always tricky. Direct sunshine on a mountain face can negatively affect conditions and increase the risk of an avalanche. We were up at higher altitudes, fatigued from climbing, on steep terrain, above the tree line or among trees; tree skiing was fun but caution was required as we worked around tree wells (where the snow lapped the base of trees) and tried not to fall in. On glaciers we had to beware of deep crevasses, which could be difficult to spot, especially for me. The eye operations of my childhood had left me with virtually no depth perception and a tendency to tired eyes.

Then there was the weather: conditions changed constantly. We'd get so hot on the climb up we'd be stripping off layers, then we'd be into the shadow of the mountain with the wind whipping us into icicles. We had to be flexible, ready for anything, on the alert—which I loved. It was the way I'd felt as a child in the North, totally alive, tuned in to nature, stimulated and challenged by my surroundings. But always, in the back of our minds, was the issue of safety. We minimized risk of injury by being in top physical condition (with strong quads). We developed our mental toughness and technical skill. However the ultimate reality was that, no matter how strong we were, we were never fully in control. The mountains were in charge.

On the descent I learned to ski deep powder by unweighting, bending my knees and lifting up as I turned from side to side, laying tracks with Brian skiing behind me in an opposite figure eight pattern, or in tandem, leaving fresh snow for others. This was the unspoken etiquette for off-piste skiing. Everyone wanted fresh tracks in powder. Untrained amateurs who didn't know what they were doing could be frustrating and dangerous, trashing the mountain in a hurry.

Skiing well in the backcountry required razor sharp coordination. It was all in the feeling, feeling the edge, loading and unloading the skis, carving the turn, weighting and unweighting as I descended a steep slope, going after the rush of speed and a consistent rhythm to my turns. I read the slope, felt the tempo of the run and changed my speed accordingly.

As I started to feel good, I "opened it up". Mental focus was critical. I was making split second decisions as the terrain changed and if I was distracted at all, I wouldn't be able to control my skis properly. That's when the worst falls occured.

How to describe the sheer beauty of the experience? It was musical, rhythmical, feeling the flow of my turns, my whole body, my entire being fully alive in the endless powder. I lost myself, all my troubles vanished in the backcountry. It was heaven. Our true religion, Brian and I discovered, was linked to our feelings about being in nature. We'd both been raised Catholic; he'd attended Brebeuf College, a Jesuit institution in Toronto, and he's a very spiritual guy—though most people just see his athletic, competitive side. Together, on skis, in the mountains, we experienced an ecstasy that I've heard some people feel when they're praying to God.

It's simple: the beauty of the mountains, the pleasure of performance, all parts working together in harmony. The rush of adrenalin. The speed, the snow, the sun. Heart pounding, senses elevated, glowing with confidence. It's like a symphony, everything happening at once. And experiencing it with someone you love—there's nothing like it. It's pure magic.

Brian helped me push myself to achieve more than I initially thought I could. He says I'm headstrong. I know he's never so alive as when he's in a high risk situation, but he's not reckless. He's knowledgeable and strong. He calculates the risks. I never feel I'm in danger with Brian. Together, we share a passion for pushing ourselves to the edge.

Our obsession with the risks and rewards of extreme skiing grew as we got better at it. I never tired of the life we were leading. We thought we were the happiest, luckiest people in the world. Our future in the Rockies was bright. At 24, Brian had secured his first real job, as a salesman for NCR Canada, a global technology firm that had a western regional office in Calgary. Within months he was enjoying the successes of a booming marketplace. This was the early 1980s and there was no place on earth like Calgary, we thought. The economy was on fire. We skied as much as our jobs allowed, from November to May. Sometimes I'd bump into Brian on the mountain on a Thursday afternoon and he'd still be wearing his Oxford cloth shirt from the office. It was hilarious—he was always looking for a quiet exit and an excuse to get into the mountains. He was quick to develop customers en route to Banff and Lake Louise.

Marriage was on Brian's mind, but the first time he mentioned it I wasn't ready. I thought we needed to travel and explore the world; I was in no rush to settle down. But in the summer of 1982, back east at the Grant family cottage, Brian told me he'd spoken to my mother—she loved Brian—and "it was officially approved," he said. We could get married, if I agreed, the following summer at the cottage. He expressed gratitude that he didn't have to ask my father for my hand in marriage. "I'd seen your father," Brian told me. "He was a very intimidating man. I'm not sure what he would have made of me, a city boy."

For our wedding on July 23, 1983, all I did was choose my dress. Mom did everything else, assisted by my sister Susan and a wedding planner from Toronto. Mom had pale pink geraniums planted all around the cottage and along the shoreline—the exact shade of pink to match the marquee tent that was erected on the cottage lawn. Susan's three small children were in the wedding party. My eldest brother Peter walked me down the aisle of the Roman Catholic Church in New Liskeard, and the guests were later transported to the cottage for a lakeside dinner. We had a live band and a pianist who played all night. The whole family came together, and to me it seemed as if the wedding was Mom's last hurrah. It may have been the happiest day of her life since the death of my father seven years earlier. It was indeed the happiest day of my life at the time.

Back in Calgary, I was on a roll, married to this absolutely dreamy guy, commuting to Lake Louise every weekend. We did lots of helicopter skiing in Revelstoke, Golden and Blue River, and hit all the hot spots in the west that were just becoming well known: Rossland, Fernie and Whistler. Brian and I had good jobs and felt we were being recognized by our peers and bosses as "high potentials." We were risk takers. Free spirits, masked by our proper business attire.

I was young. I didn't yet understand the inevitability of life's ups and downs. Nothing ever stays the same—but it took quite a pounding for me to get the message. Less than six months after the wedding, Brian accepted a promotion and transfer to NCR's Toronto office. I was happy for him and devastated for myself. The opportunity was too great for Brian to resist; clearly if he was to make it at NCR, he had to get on the fast track at the Canadian head office.

I resigned from what I thought was the world's greatest job and, with no plans in sight, moved to Toronto. I left behind all my friends, business contacts and my heavenly life in the mountains. We settled into a rented house in downtown Toronto, but the sacrifice of leaving the mountains was close to unbearable, and I was unable to express my feelings to anyone. Brian started playing hockey in a men's league but I felt no desire to make a new life for myself. This was one of the most difficult and lonely stages of my adult life. In the mountains, I'd felt whole, but back in the city, a dark feeling descended, an emptiness that echoed with memories of my father's death. Once again, I was consumed with an enormous sense of loss.

An exciting and challenging new work environment stimulated my husband but I was unemployed, lacking a sense of purpose or direction. I felt as if I had been robbed. I regretted the big-hearted decision to support my husband's career. Even though two-career families are more common today, it is still a difficult decision to make, when one partner gets a job offer and the other doesn't necessarily want to move. Nowadays the highest money-earner normally gets priority, but back in the early 80's it seemed only right to make the decision based on the husband's work only. The wife's career didn't count for as much. I guess it was expected that she would eventually start a family and focus on that. She would adjust.

Brian shared my yearning for the mountains and during our first winter in Toronto, we decided to ski the Swiss and French Alps. The winter of '85 was a great snow year for Europe and we took full advantage. We flew to Zurich and traveled mostly by train to six different resorts, including Zermatt, Verbier, Chamonix, Val d'Isere and Courchevel. We stayed in old-style mountain ski hotels, ate Swiss muesli for breakfast, stashed Swiss chocolate in our packs and at night gorged on goulash and fondue. I wore a flashy hot pink "Powdergirl" ski suit that startled the Brits in Verbier; they'd never seen anything like it, when I came bombing down in deep powder. They loved to tease "the Canadian." They were in disbelief that a woman in fluorescent pink could be so aggressive. We had a ball. We'd race down for the last run of the day and ski to the train station, arriving just as the train was pulling out. We'd jump on the train in our ski boots, skis over our shoulders, laughing and throwing our packs on top. What makes a marriage strong? These shared moments, these memories.

I began to think Toronto wasn't so bad after all—a direct flight to Zurich took just a little longer than flying across Canada to Calgary and driving up to Banff. And when we got back, I had a job—thanks to my sister Susan. She introduced me to a friend who ran a small industrial psychology consulting firm. Jackson & Smye wanted a marketing director to help the firm expand, sell the concept of executive coaching and grow into the U.S market. The focus was professional services marketing, about as far as one could get from world famous ski-area marketing, but I went for it because it was the only offer I had. "Work with what you've got," I was told, so I did, even though I wasn't overly enthusiastic. But I learned a lot. Let's just say it was never fun; selling human resources and improved hiring practices from a group of shrinks to HR departments was not going to cut it, long term, for me. I loved the partners, but we were like oil and water. They wanted to talk about feelings and I wanted to get things done. They'd worry about how to formulate strategic approaches. I'd say, "It's really simple, guys, you make 40 phone calls a day, you get maybe 10 people who'll talk to you, you get five appointments and if you're lucky you get two new clients."

I helped the firm grow close to 65% in the first year and they opened an office in the U.S. I was golden, but unfulfilled. I missed my job in the Rocky Mountains. My casual dress-code of Bogner ski pants and fur hats, skiing 140 days a year, hardly compared to riding the crowded TTC subway to work in my best blue wool suit. Out of my natural habitat, I was uptight. Sensing my unhappiness, my bosses—both registered psychologists—tried to get me to talk about my feelings. Which I wasn't good at. In their efforts to lift my spirits, they widened the scope of my job. I gave speeches to the American Marketing Association and to professional services firms—doctors, lawyers and accountants—in the U.S. I persevered, but I wasn't turned on, professionally.

On the home front, Brian and I were getting into a groove—so much so, in fact, that we were thrilled when, after two years of marriage, we found out I was expecting a baby. Our beloved son, Hudson, was born on July 12, 1986. He was a beautiful, easy baby and settled in very quickly. Four weeks later, I was back at work. *Baby's healthy, baby's feeding, baby's sleeping*, I thought—and saw no particular use for myself in staying home. I nursed him morning and night and pumped milk for bottles during the day. Tammy, the eldest daughter of a large family from New Liskeard, moved in to look after Hudson while I was at work; the baby was in better hands with her than me, I figured, since she had so much experience looking after children. And I felt comfortable with her because she was from the North. (She stayed two years and went on to Queen's University.)

But I was blindsided by the emotional pull of wanting to be with the baby. I wasn't expecting to be torn, but as much as I needed the stimulation of work, I wanted to spend time with Hudson. This was the beginning of a long struggle in my search for balance. I was afraid of living a narrow life circumscribed by domesticity. I didn't want to be trapped at home. Brian was a parent—a loving, devoted father—and his life was going on more or less as usual. Why should my life change dramatically? No one said, "Maybe you should stay at home with the baby a little longer, maybe you'll be too exhausted nursing a baby and recovering from childbirth, maybe the baby needs you." None of these propositions occurred to me. I was needed at the office. I wanted to work.

I guess I must have felt invincible. I'd always been a strong and healthy athlete and suddenly, I was tired and weak. My body ached. I'd sit at my desk and feel as if I couldn't get up. I couldn't understand what was happening to me. I had trouble getting out of bed in the morning. Then I got really sick, I lost weight, I was exhausted, my temperature was elevated and the search was on to diagnose what ailed me. Doctors thought I had strep throat, then it was ulcers, mononucleosis, and hepatitis. For six months, I languished, secretly convinced I had leukemia. Brian's father and uncle had both died of leukemia. My symptoms, especially the deep exhaustion, seemed to mimic leukemia. My doctor tested me for every disease under the sun. The day he called me with the results, I was too weak to drive to his office and took a taxi. I sat in his office, sobbing, a bag of bones, thinking, *He's going to tell me I have leukemia. I know it. I'm dying.*

When he said, "You have this rare virus, Epstein-Barr, otherwise known as Chronic Fatigue Syndrome," I was elated even though I didn't know what it was. He must have been startled by my almost giddy reaction. "There's not much we can do," he went on, "your white blood cell count is a little high, but basically, you just have to rest." I wasn't dying!

It was just a virus, not leukemia! The fear I'd built up over six months was gone. I began to recover immediately.

I realized I'd been trying to live up to my father's high standards and expectations of peak performance. The physical and emotional strain of doing it all—being a loving mother to a newborn baby, going for it at work—had made me sick, had broken down my immune system. The culture of my family when I was growing up was so male dominated it hadn't occurred to me that a woman's needs could be different. I had serious aspirations of becoming the chief executive officer of a major corporation—that's how I was wired. I thought I was going all the way to the top. Baby or not, there was no stopping me. Success and achievement at all costs, that's the message I'd absorbed, as a child. I believed I could have it all—a great family, loving relationships, fantastic job, career success.

I'd read the baby books but ignored, or couldn't relate to, the advice about the need for rest after childbirth, the need to take the time to bond with your baby. I carried on. Nobody talked to me about all the hormones and the emotional side of giving birth and the exhaustion factor. I thought you were supposed to soldier on. Even if my mother had said, "Stay home with the baby," would I have listened? Brian says I'm headstrong; I wasn't asking for help.

Shortly after the Epstein-Barr diagnosis, I flew to Bermuda with my mother for a week, to lie on the beach and rest, and my symptoms began to disappear. The day after we returned, a headhunter called. American Express was interested in talking to me. A week later, I joined the American Express marketing team in Canada and my career path took a turn upward. I was back on track with a big league brand, a truly marketing-driven organization. I could not have been more excited. But I had more hard lessons to learn.

CHAPTER FIVE

Struggle for Balance

1987-2004

WHEN YOU'RE LIVING THROUGH different stages of your life, you don't know you're in "a stage," and you're not fully aware of what's happening. You don't know what you don't know. So it was for me during the next decade and a half. The pressures built up as the old balancing act got ever more complicated and I tried to find a path through the maze.

I was a perfectionist. No amount of effort was ever good enough. The drive and ambition I had was so deeply rooted that it ruled me. I did it all: Work, motherhood, being a dedicated wife, moving back and forth across the country six times to accommodate my husband's rise up the corporate ladder, setting myself up in business as a consultant, living in and renovating 14 homes in three different cities—Toronto, Calgary and Vancouver—AND finding time to ski. Extreme skiing was the most fulfilling aspect of my life, next to my family, but it wasn't something I could do every day. To give ourselves a base, Brian and I bought a house outside Vancouver at Whistler (the site of the 2010 Winter Olympics). We worked to ski and saved up our holiday time (and money) so that we could spend every spare moment in the mountains.

Back in Toronto, I started working at American Express in 1987. I was 30 years old, married to a man I loved, mother of a beautiful baby boy, and for the first time since I'd left the Rocky Mountains, I was engaged in work I genuinely loved with a dynamic team of people. I couldn't see anything holding me back. I watched my husband ascend the corporate ladder. Surely a similar future would await me, given the same hard work. It didn't quite happen that way. Life is different for women—but I didn't know.

Debra Isenberg was my inspiration at Amex. One of the top female executives in the U.S.—she was ranked by Fortune magazine, a notable distinction in the male-dominated corporate world—Debra came up from the U.S. to run marketing at Amex Canada. We clicked. She was the first senior woman I'd worked with whom I really admired. She was bright and real and eager to share her knowledge. She could crunch numbers in her head. One day she came out of her office and walked over to my cubicle. "If you ever need a babysitter for Hudson," she said, "I'd be delighted to help out." I was touched. I was having trouble juggling—the job, getting home for Hudson, taking care of domestic issues—while performing well in a demanding position that required considerable travel. I hadn't realized she was aware of the balancing act. (Like most senior women, she didn't have children.)

Amex was an exciting place to be in the 1980s. We had big budgets to spend on marketing financial services, charge cards and travel offices, and launching strategic partnerships to promote Amex. There was "Front of the Line," various rewards programs, the Platinum Card, and the Canadian launch of *Phantom of the Opera*. I had a sense of purpose, professionally, which gave me a feeling of belonging. My colleagues were creative thinkers. I loved having access to the New York offices and the innovation that was going on in the U.S. I felt charged up again! And my initiatives were being recognized. I experienced some big wins and was awaiting a promised directorship.

Then there was our skiing. Brian and I went hard at it in the French, Swiss and Italian Alps as well as at Whistler. We had wonderful holidays to Cortina, Klosters, Davos, St. Anton and Chamonix. In 1989 we returned to Val d'Isere and took Hudson, who was three. My eldest brother Peter and his children, plus my two younger brothers joined us. We enrolled Hudson in Le Petit Poussette, a learn-to-ski program for nursery-aged children. Brian would go down the mountain to get him at lunch and bring him up to ski with us at high altitudes. Hudson took it all in stride. He was amusing, a tiny little guy in a down-filled ski suit and helmet, trying to ski and be part of the extended family. He was really good.

One day, Brian and I joined a 90-mile trek led by our guide, Jacques, through the Trois Vallee. We skied through farmers' fields and pastures and up into the French Alps. It was exquisitely beautiful and historic but very tough. Of the twelve skiers who started out, only four finished. I was the only female. The physical demands of completing the trip were intense and it was a huge accomplishment for me. I loved the sense of exploring a vast landscape, of not being confined. It was like being in the North. I couldn't have been happier.

But back at home storm clouds were gathering on the work front and I was too busy to notice. Establishing myself on the fast track within the deadly competitive environment at Amex, I developed "working mother's guilt" big time. There was a constant battle within me, a struggle every day leaving my son, whom I loved, to go to work, which I loved. What was wrong with this picture? Why didn't Brian feel torn apart? Was there something wrong with me? I'd be working frantically on a project at the office, watching the clock, trying to get home to take Hudson to the doctor—we had a live-in nanny, but I didn't want her to completely assume the parenting role—and felt I couldn't tell my colleagues that I had a commitment to my child. (Few of them had children; if they did, I didn't hear about it.) I thought I'd be penalized if I couldn't put in the same hours, didn't demonstrate the same level of dedication. But even stronger than the peer pressure was the old programming—the internalized demands for perfection, the tape that kept playing in my head. Do it all. Have it all. Go after it all. In fact, I was doing too much and verging on burn out. I was exhausted and starting to lose that zest for life, that fire for work.

"My mind reels with it," Anne Morrow Lindbergh wrote in *Gift from the Sea*. "What a circus act we women perform every day of our lives…We must be open to all points of the compass: husband, children, friends, home, community; stretched out, exposed, sensitive like a spider's web to each breeze that blows, to each call that comes. How difficult for us, then, to achieve a balance in the midst of these contradictory tensions, and yet how necessary for the proper functioning of our lives." That's how I felt, like a web reaching in all directions, stretched to the limit.

One day the nanny was held up at the Canada-U.S. border, returning from a trip to Buffalo, and Hudson said, "I've lost my mother." He wasn't even three years old. I was devastated, and decided on the spot: no more live-in nannies. If we were going to be parents, we had to find another way. At the same time, my mother's health began to fail. And there were decisions to be made about the family business up North. Since the concept of including the females actively in day-to-day operations was never a consideration, I couldn't participate in finding solutions. All I could do was worry. The pressures were overwhelming.

I resigned from Amex—a truly wrenching decision; my boss was surprised, given my obvious ambition—and headed for the cottage on Twin Lakes. I wanted to keep a watchful eye on my mother and give my son a summer like the ones I'd loved growing up. But I was tortured by the ongoing battle to balance my desire for a fulfilling career while caring for my family. Was I giving up when I should soldier on? Amex tried to convince me take a leave of absence but I knew in my gut I couldn't continue with the level of corporate pressure and confinement that was necessary if I was going for the top. In leaving Amex, I'd made the first decision that was truly mine, that came from my heart, that shocked me, in a way. It wasn't Brian or my family pushing me to do something. It was my choice to step back. I was amazed that I could.

Yet when I returned to Toronto that fall, rested and refreshed, I was still wrestling with the same questions. Should I pursue a career or set myself up at home and try to balance a small business part-time with family full-time? Would I sell myself short if I gave up corporate life? Would I ever be happy with anything less? Would my precious son Hudson and my husband Brian lose out if I revived my ambitions? The old tape kept playing and there was no one to talk to, no mother's group, no sharing of "war stories" among professional women. We were so isolated from each other back then—or at least I was. The role modeling I'd had from birth was clear: drive for the top and love your spouse and family and happiness will follow. It had worked for my father—but then, he had died young, at 55, even though he had a wonderful wife to look after him. Could stress have played a part?

Before I had time to make a decision, Brian was offered another corporate promotion that included a transfer back to Calgary, this time as vice president of NCR Canada. We ran at the chance to be close to the mountains. It was an instantaneous decision. This time around, I knew what to do, professionally: I pursued a consulting career in advertising and marketing strategy. With big name experience at American Express and so many partnership-marketing programs under my belt, I felt confident working with clients in Calgary. This was a turning point for me. I could be my own boss and manage my own business. I carved out a niche for myself that was intellectually stimulating and financially rewarding, providing marketing advice and strategic advertising support for presidents and vice-presidents of major publicly-traded companies and national banks.

The second run in Calgary was great. We skied and hiked at Lake Louise every weekend when we weren't going to Whistler; the Calgary Flames were winning and Hudson started to play hockey at the outdoor arena at Elbow Park with the wooden goalies. (The shape of a goalie was positioned in the center of each goal so that all the kids could learn to skate.) I loved being back at the rink, watching hockey. Business was good, skiing was awesome and I was on a roll as a consultant. With easy access to the mountains, we were relaxed again. I felt I could live in the moment. It was like returning to the North.

I thought I had it all. At 35 I was happy, successful, enjoying being a mother, wife, daughter, sister, volunteer and friend. I felt more balanced. I was close to nature and achieving my goals. I was independent. I was earning a solid living and maintaining a strong family life. We bought a beautiful home on the escarpment with views of the mountains and gave Hudson his first Lab puppy. The crowded TTC subway was just a distant memory.

Two short years in Calgary came to an abrupt end when Brian was transferred to Vancouver. He was moving up the ladder and I was forced to be ever more creative about my career. I sold our Calgary home, searched for a new one in Vancouver, did the usual shut-down and set-up, found a good school for Hudson and figured out where to buy groceries and get my hair cut. The great advantage of this posting was our closeness to Whistler. Then I found out I was pregnant. Hudson would soon turn 9 and I was 37 years old. My doctor ordered an amniocentesis because of my age. Afterward, I bled internally and was supposed to stay in bed for six weeks, which meant I couldn't ski, but I accompanied Brian and Hudson up to Whistler. I'd stand around the base of the mountain waiting for them—and waiting for the result of the amnio. It turned out to be a false positive. The suggestion of "high risk" was wrong; the baby was perfectly fine. But it was a worrying process I had to cope with while Brian lived in Dayton, Ohio for five months, spending time at NCR's U.S. headquarters, coming back to Vancouver every second weekend.

I had been working hard to make contacts and re-launch myself as an independent consultant, and was just getting going when Brian was asked to relocate back to Toronto, where he would eventually become president of NCR Canada. It was the kind of promotion he couldn't turn down if he wanted to continue the upward momentum. We hadn't been in Vancouver for a full year. Corporate life was getting difficult to predict. The stress of so many moves had taken a toll and I wasn't looking forward to the next one, away from the mountains. I would have to restart my career all over again in Toronto. These were opportunities for Brian—but not for me. Every move represented a challenge I had to overcome in my professional life.

Starting all over again with every move is tiresome—especially when it's a corporate move—and as women who've been through it know, the work usually falls to the female. We had bought and renovated 12 houses at this point, lived in each one while under construction, sold it after approximately a year, then started the process all over again. This particular move was really tough. I would soon turn 38, I was eight months pregnant and I was drained. Out of gas.

We arrived in Toronto one month before Hilary was born on September 6, 1994. She was an adorable baby, easy to care for, and I was flooded with love and a sense of poignancy and time passing. I knew I wouldn't have this experience again. I felt vulnerable but couldn't admit it, didn't have the language to talk about my feelings or my needs. There was work to be done and I dove in. We were settling into a new house, unpacking boxes and figuring out where to put things, getting back into the Toronto grind, and adjusting routines to welcome our second child. I hired a night nurse to stay at the house for the first few months, as I'd done with Hudson. The nurse sat in a rocking chair, close to the baby's bassinet, and if Hilary woke up, the nurse came to get me so I could feed the baby. This enabled me to go back to work within six weeks of giving birth.

Brian's life carried on; mine should have too. I felt blessed to have two wonderful children and a husband who was dedicated to us, but I was still searching, still driven. Women were pressured to "put family first"—and I did—but I wasn't ashamed to say I loved to work. And a great opportunity presented itself: Visa Canada was looking for someone to fill in on a maternity leave. (Visa Canada has a progressive maternity leave policy that gives its female staff excellent support. It didn't occur to me that I should be on an extended maternity leave myself.) I started a consulting assignment that developed into an on-going business relationship that has continued for many years. But the juggling act intensified. Brian was heading up NCR Canada, and the corporate demands escalated for entertaining and attending charitable functions. He needed "the wife" by his side for many of these events, and we always managed to have fun together. But it was a lot. We had to be out doing corporate socializing a couple of times a week, we kept up an intense pace at work full-time, looked after our children and volunteered in the community. Plus skiing, which remained our true passion, our escape, our chance to live on the edge.

At Christmas, we flew to Whistler for the holidays, with a three-month-old baby and Hudson, a nine year old in grade three, with a nanny and a dog. It was a relief to escape Toronto and return to the place that felt like our real home. Friends came to visit but they didn't quite "get" what we did in the mountains. Not many people in our social or corporate circles were into long mountain climbs outside the boundary ropes carrying a heavy pack, then skiing down in fresh powder for runs that lasted 20 to 30 minutes. Our friends preferred chairlifts and groomed runs, which was fine with us. We were up at 7:30 in the morning, eating our porridge, checking weather reports, packing water and a little Swiss milk chocolate for energy. Occasionally Brian put an orange in, for a treat. Outfitted in our favourite gear—me in my white Bogner ski suit and a Chanel helmet, Brian in his Prada suit—we climbed together to reach the summit, looking like "chalet skiers" in our fancy ski clothes. The extreme skiing fanatics, young guys in torn, duck-taped Gore-Tex suits, couldn't believe their eyes. They were like surfer dudes, hotdoggers who belonged to an exclusive club, who lived for their sport and traveled the world, from one hot spot to the next. They stared at us. *How'd you get here? Drop down from Mars?* Then we'd rip down the face of the mountain. We earned their respect. (Secretly, we wanted to be part of their scene.)

The great thing about Whistler was its massive terrain and easy-to-reach backcountry, which enabled us to do three or four loops a day, sometimes climbing up three or four times, often not stopping for lunch. I never liked to ski the same line twice on the same day. Every experience was different. But there was a painful side—there always is, to any intense sport—involving feet and shins rubbed raw from climbing in stiff ski boots. I'd have to tape my feet and shins with moleskin; most mornings before we headed to the mountain, I'd soak in a scalding hot bath with Epsom salts to loosen up my muscles from the exertions of the day before. And I had to watch out for my heart. It tended to race in high altitudes and doctors had warned me to be careful. I also had to deal with numbness in my hands and feet, caused by slower circulation resulting from less oxygen in the cold mountain air at high elevations.

Brian and I were very much a unit, happy to ski on our own and with our children as they got older. When Hilary was two, she went down a hill at Blackcomb on her first pair of skis, between our legs. Hudson was climbing with us when he was six. In grade two, when he was seven years old, he climbed the Spearhead Glacier at Whistler for the first time. Before he'd hit his teenage years, he was skiing off-piste with Brian and I on a regular basis.

One day Hudson heard someone at a party in Toronto say, "The Sullivans like to ski," and he thought: *People don't understand what we do, the passion with which we go into the backcountry and ski the steeps.* He realized that, for his family, skiing was a unifying force. "For a ton of people, skiing is a social thing, a recreational thing, hanging out at the chalet," he told me. "That's not what we do." I had to laugh, caught up in the memory of the scorn we had heaped, as children, on "chalet skiers" up North.

It was all about choices. I never became skilled in the domestic arts, though I admire women who are. I wasn't very interested in cooking—one of the reasons I worked so hard was to be able to afford a cook—and I couldn't sew. If buttons fell off, Brian sewed them on. I was bent on not joining the "desperate housewives" brigade—women at home with their kids, bored out of their minds. I knew women like that, and I felt for them. The way I figured it, we've all got a limited amount of energy, and I'd chosen to focus mine where it counted most. I wanted to get the biggest bang for my buck. I didn't want to grow old thinking about all the things I wished I'd done. It can be hard stepping out of the stereotypes assigned to one's gender, female or male, but fulfillment, I'd found, came from following my deepest urges and instincts. Curiously, I was sometimes questioned about my passion for off piste skiing. It was suggested, occasionally, that perhaps I pursued it because of my husband. That he "pushed" me to do it. I politely demolished such assumptions, privately annoyed by the subtext—that a woman, left to her own devices, wouldn't want to do anything as rigorous as backcountry skiing. It's true that not many women do it, but there are lots of things women haven't had the opportunity to try. I was incredibly fortunate to have been brought up in the North with no barriers to my physical pursuits. As well, I'd been raised to achieve and excel and take risks. My parents were such extraordinary characters that I grew up believing I could do anything. Women don't have to be trapped in a straitjacket. Life doesn't have to be easy to be enjoyable. My happiness came from being true to my roots—though some mediation was required, I would learn.

Daily life was hectic. Hudson was enrolled at Upper Canada College in Form One and I went into over-drive. I spent my days in meetings involving Visa Canada, its Olympic sponsorship, and English and French print and TV advertising. Despite having a new baby at home and a new house to organize, I also volunteered at Hudson's school, co-chairing committees and sitting on the executive of the parents' organization over a 10-year span. These "invisible" volunteer jobs, which are done mainly by women and are the lifeblood of many organizations, eat up a huge amount of time, requiring evening meetings and lots of fundraising activities. And I had to take Hudson to soccer, hockey and tennis practice. As well, the gap in age between Hilary and Hudson meant spending a lot of individual time with each child; they were at such different stages. Brian tried his best to be with them as much as he could, but the demands of his job put enormous pressure on him. Even so, I always felt he was there for us when we needed him most.

I'd be up part of the night nursing Hilary and trying to settle her down, then catch a 5:30 am limousine to the airport for the first morning flight to Montreal. I would sleep in the back of the car and Steve, my driver, would wake me when we reached Pearson International Airport. I'd find my way onto the aircraft and sleep for the 45-minute flight to Dorval. Sometimes I'd be in meetings and notice baby spit-up on the shoulder of my pin-stripe suit. Yet I enjoyed managing the fierce pace of meetings, budgets, boardroom presentations and persuading bankers to invest more in marketing the brand. I was effective, I think—as many women are—because I had no time to waste. I'd get to the point, bring people together and build relationships to achieve a win-win for everyone. But I didn't hang around. I was in and out. I had baby Hilary at home to nurse so I'd return to Toronto at the end of the day.

Looking in the rear-view mirror, I see this period in my life as one of tremendous growth and change. The pace was intense, the amount of business travel excessive, the work highly stimulating—and it was always rewarding to return home to my loving family. The media reflected, I thought, what I was living. Designer Donna Karan came out with a series of ads of women in power suits, strutting downtown, looking glamorous and authoritative. The message was clear: women could have it all, work hard, have gorgeous families and fulfilling careers. It was a fantasy, but I made a run for it. I perspired through meetings to get to teacher interviews and school plays. I drove my car like a maniac at break-neck speed to make it to my son's hockey game before it ended. I may have cut clients off when I was exasperated and short of time. I hosted parties for charities, neighbours, friends and family. I entertained visiting executives for both my own and my husband's business purposes. I volunteered and supervised tutoring programs in math and reading for inner city school children every Wednesday from 4:30 to 6 pm. Brian and I, with Hudson and Hilary, co-founded a charity, Young Friends of Sick Children's Hospital, to supply books, music and toys to children in need of comfort after a serious operation. I had been a patient at Sick Kids when I was a child, undergoing eye surgery, and I knew how lonely and scary it could be.

I'm not complaining. I did it all happily—but over time it became exhausting. Organizing domestic life became increasingly complicated as the children got older. I'd be running flat out all weekend, keeping up with their activities, only to get up early Monday morning, do my workout before the children got up, and head to the office. (Since the late 1980s I'd recognized the need to be in constant training for backcountry skiing.) I knew I couldn't keep going like this. Something was going to give, and it was going to be me.

Then I had a breakthrough—before I got sick. Due to renew my contract with Visa Canada, I told the senior vice president that I was planning to scale down my consulting assignment from five days a week to three days, to spend more time with my children. I felt some trepidation. Did he think it would work? Yes, he said, absolutely. He was very supportive. Would Visa sideline me? Would the company invade my "off time?" No, they respected my decision and structured the job so that I was able to grow professionally while sticking religiously to a Tuesday, Wednesday, Thursday work week. I arrived at the office at 8:30 am, didn't take lunch, didn't look up, and left at 6 pm sharp. ("Pay me for three days and I'll give you five days worth of work," was what I essentially said. And my day rate, already at a senior professional level of compensation, went up.)

I learned about microchip technology and, on behalf of Visa Canada, worked with the major banks to explore the possibility of replacing the magnetic stripe with a microchip that contained a more enhanced form of security. This was the "Smart Card" that is so popular in Europe today. I spearheaded three pilots of this technology in the mid 1990s in Montreal, Toronto and Vancouver. The project, Visa Cash, financed by Visa International out of San Francisco, is an electronic purse that will undoubtedly become a widely used form of transaction in the future.

Through it all, Brian and I were devoted mountain skiers, commuting to our home at Whistler for Christmas, Easter, March break, long weekends, and the months of July and August. (Brian had an office in Vancouver which made it possible to work from the West Coast.) In summer, we hiked and went fly fishing on the Squamish River. Hilary and I picked berries in the Pemberton Valley while Brian and Hudson skied the glaciers. The Whistler summers were like being at the cottage in the North. The solitude, the wilderness, the peace and quiet, the beauty of our surroundings—just like my childhood paradise. But it went further than that, more than just the closeness to nature. It was the mountains, the adrenalin rush of skiing the steeps.

The longer we did it, the more aware we became of the risks. In the mornings, I learned to listen for the sound of avalanche bombs—explosives detonated to release the snow buildup in dangerous areas. In a state of heightened alertness, I watched the weather, the snowpack, changes of terrain as we descended; I was aware of gathering clouds, shifts in wind and snow conditions, sudden temperature drops. Danger was ever present, regardless of how experienced and skilled we were. I had a friend who was killed in an avalanche, years ago in Banff. He was a trained, licensed mountain guide. You think it will never happen to you.

Once, I was skiing alone. Brian and Hudson had gone ahead and I was exploring the terrain further out. Traversing across a ridge, looking for a good powder line, I ended up trapped on a high, narrow, dead end cliff outside the Whistler boundary. The precipice was about 12 inches wide, with a treacherous, 60-foot drop. I couldn't see to back up because of my eye problem. Able to only see out of one eye at a time, I was terrified I would misread the terrain and step into the void. After a few "Hail Marys," I finally mustered the courage to make the move. Standing on my left ski, I quickly lifted my right ski and turned it in a semi-circle pointing to my back. Then I had to carefully place my left ski around parallel to the right. If I missed the scissorkick, I would be off the cliff. After much heart-pounding angst, I got up my nerve, made the move and got out unscathed. I skied straight down to the base and went to the little Catholic church in Whistler, Our Lady of the Mountains, where I kneeled and thanked God for my safety. The lesson I had learned in the North—never swim alone—was reinforced. Don't ski alone in the backcountry, ever.

When Hudson was 12, speed skiing with his dad on the Saudan Couloir, the steepest pitch in-bounds on Blackcomb, he plummeted from top to bottom, about 400 yards, tumbling head over heels. He lost everything, skis, poles, goggles, helmet—but apart from some bruising he wasn't seriously injured. No broken bones. "It was a big wake up call, though," he told me later. "It was very scary, being totally out of control." Over time, Hudson became more cautious when he skied the steeps at high speed with his father. "When I'm with Dad, I'm the voice of reason. It's not that he pushes me, it's just that he's very adventurous. I'm more like Dad when I'm with my friends—that's when I'm the one who likes to go to the edge. When Dad skis with other people, he's more conscious of their limits, he caters to their needs. I think that's why he loves to ski with me and Mom, because he can go to the edge with us. We can enjoy it with him."

When Hudson was 13, near the end of a long, hard day of skiing with his father, they decided to climb the Spearhead Glacier. On the descent, Brian had an accident, a bad crash, and broke one of his skis. The other ski fell into a crevasse. Without skis, there was no way for him to get out of the valley. It was four p.m. and the sun was setting. I was at home with Hilary, who was only four, waiting for them, getting anxious as the sky turned black. I sensed something was wrong. Shortly after 6 pm, I called the mountain to report my husband and son missing. The patrol policy at the time was to wait 24 hours for missing persons to potentially show up before embarking on a full search and rescue mission. I was afraid Brian and Hudson had had a terrible accident and weren't coming back. It was mid-winter, with temperatures dropping from -10°C to -20°C. They would never make it through the night. There was nothing for me to do but wait and pray.

At 8 pm, Brian and Hudson finally staggered in, exhausted. There was not a lot of conversation. Obviously Brian had had an accident. They went to bed. Over the next few days, they told me what had happened: while trying to retrieve his unbroken ski, Brian dropped into the crevasse and couldn't climb out. The interior was solid ice and he didn't have any ropes or an ice pick. He was down so deep Hudson couldn't reach him. "I felt useless, worthless, watching him struggle down there," Hudson said. "I didn't think, *Dad will die*, but I was scared."

After more than an hour trying to climb up the ice wall, Brian told Hudson to start skiing out before it got too dark. Hudson refused to leave his father. There was a great deal of tension. Brian thought he might not make it but he didn't tell Hudson that. Finally, nearing physical exhaustion, Brian found a way to wedge his skis into the ice wall, one at time, and leveraged himself up. With a huge adrenalin rush, he pulled himself onto the edge of the crevasse, where Hudson was able to haul him over. Their bond was cemented then and there. Hudson was just a kid, a tough little guy, and he probably saved his father's life.

"My Dad is my skiing buddy," Hudson said. "Yeah, he skis fast, drives fast, thinks fast, but that's not his personality at home. He's actually a very subtle person. He doesn't talk about his wild and crazy skiing exploits. That's not how he approaches it. I'm not scared when I ski with him. It's the opposite."

Did Brian take unnecessary risks? Was he being careless? No, I don't think so. Risk is part of the sport of off piste skiing. It's not for the faint of heart. If you aren't experienced and don't understand what you're doing, you shouldn't be out there. "Extreme skiing can be very dangerous," Brian said. "If you're physically strong and mentally tough, you can find your way out of scary situations. You have to draw on all your resources. If you're not prepared for that, don't go." That's what he loves, the thrill of being pushed to the edge. Fear makes him smarter, quicker, more alive. That's when Brian's eyes start to dance.

But for me, by 2004 a different kind of fear seeped into my life. Hudson was 17 going on 18—the same age I'd been when my father died—and something odd came over me. I had been haunted by my father's death, and an enormous sense of loss, for so long. Was it now returning, casting its dark shadow over me?

P.J. Grant's first sawmill, Latchford, *1920's*

The 11 Grant children at home with our parents.
I am standing front-row center, *1962*

My father, John Morgan Grant, *1972*

With my father, *1974*

Performing at the New Liskeard
Skating Carnival, *1972*

Our Wedding, *1983*

With Brian, Hudson and my mother,
Gertrude Grant, Twin Lakes, *1988*

In my Powdergirl Suit with 205 cm skis
in Verbier, Switzerland, *1985*

Brian and I corporate entertaining,
1991

With baby Hilary and Hudson,
1994

Evolution of cash

Wednesday, December 13, 1995

Smart card buys little things in life

By Brian Lewis
Staff Reporter

"Will that be real cash . . . or plastic cash?"

If a trial launched yesterday by Visa and Vancouver City Savings Credit Union is successful, questions such as this will be commonplace for consumers in the not-too-distant future.

They'll be able to use yet another piece of plastic to replace old-fashioned folding money and coinage. But this one doesn't give credit, nor does it debit your bank account.

It's . . . well, it's cash.

But it comes in the form of a microchip-based stored value smart card called Visa Cash, that is designed for consumer purchases of $10 or less at outlets such as fast food and video shops, public transit, newspaper boxes, newsstands, pay parking lots and any other retail situations where small amounts of exact change are usually needed.

The card will have a face value denomination, for example, $20, and is used at the point-of-purchase with a specially equipped terminal which transfers the purchase value to the retailer.

Here's how it works: You purchase your $20 Visa Cash card from VanCity for exactly $20. You nip into McDonald's and buy a hamburger, fries and a drink for a total of $5.75. You present the Visa Cash card and the server punches $5.75 into the terminal.

A window on your side of the terminal shows the $5.75 purchase as well as the remaining balance on your card, but the server can't see it. You either accept the transaction or reject it. A paper receipt is issued with the transaction.

"The trial signals the beginning of a new stage in the ongoing evolution of cash," said Bob Quart, VanCity's chief executive officer.

"The card itself is just like cash."

It also means that if you lose a fresh $20 Cash card it's just like losing a crisp, new $20 bill.

VanCity is issuing the card in $5 denominations to its 250 staff in the credit union's new head office in Vancouver as well as to other staff.

Later, $20 cards will be available and ultimately they could be available in denominations of up to $500. Any small balances on an old card would be credited when you purchase a new card.

A number of retailers in the local office area, such as McDonald's, Starbucks, Subway, City Stop and Science World cafeteria and gift shop are being used in the trial.

Similar tests were launched yesterday in Toronto and Quebec by Toronto Dominion Bank, Scotiabank and Les caisses Desjardins.

"Our market research has convinced us that Canadian consumers are ready for this kind of small denomination card," says Carol Grant Sullivan of Visa Canada.

"We don't see much of an overlap between credit cards and cash cards. In Canada, there's a $75-billion market for consumer purchases of $10 or less."

She said that this is the first step in cash card development. A reloadable cash card, which could be re-filled from a bank account at an automated teller machine, is being tested in San Francisco. The disposable cash card may be available to the public by spring.

Bob Quart and Carol Grant Sullivan buy burgers using cash card.

Staff photo by David Clark

Making front page news,
The Province, Vancouver, *1995*

Our family together on
Blackcomb Mountain, *1998*

Hilary greeting Their Royal Highnesses
The Earl & Countess of Wessex
(Edward and Sophie) at RCYC, *2002*

Hudson, UCC Varsity Hockey
Team, *2004 Champions*

Summer on the Cheakamus River, Whistler, *2003*

limbing with Kees, backcountry, Andes, *2003*

Brian and I on the Summit, Andes, *2003*

Returning to the mountains, after the accident and 4 months of physical rehabilitation, Italian Alps, Courmayeur, *2005*

CHAPTER SIX

The Turning Point

Heading to the Andes

Summer of 2004

IF YOU'VE BEEN TRAUMATIZED in childhood, watch out when your child reaches the same age you were when the trauma occurred. I wasn't conscious of the connection at the time, but as Hudson entered his last year of high school, I was overwhelmed with powerful emotions. I'd never forgotten the impact of my father's death during the year I was getting ready to leave home to go to university, uncertain about my future. It was a dreadful memory: needing my father's support and direction, going to see him in the hospital, anticipating words of wisdom, getting nothing. The lifelong feeling of being shortchanged was not something I wanted to pass on to Hudson. It was an incredible pull, this desire to help, advise, and support him as much as humanly possible.

It wasn't up for discussion. I told Visa Canada I wouldn't be available for the next eight months and turned my energies to home and Hudson. Determined to ensure that this turning point in his life was positive, I might have gone a little overboard. "Hey Mom, you can get therapy for this problem," Hudson would joke. "Quit showing up at hockey practice."

I insisted that Brian attend all of Hudson's Varsity hockey games with me. Even 9-year-old Hilary got into the act. We were our own team of fans like Hudson had never seen before. We traveled to watch all his away games, as far afield as Boston, Massachusetts and Culver, Indiana. We yelled and cheered as Hudson's Upper Canada College team had a record-breaking season. Each time Hudson stepped on the ice, I was so proud of him. He'd missed out on a lot of hockey practice in previous years, because he'd devoted so much time to skiing with his family, but he'd made up for it with hard work, had been selected for the team and contributed to its success. I also enjoyed reliving my youth—all the old memories of growing up in the North flooded back, watching hours of hockey at the rink while my brothers played.

Hudson and I agonized over course selections—or maybe it was just me doing the agonizing—and pondered the pros and cons of American vs. British vs. Canadian schools. In the end he applied to all three countries and I was consumed with supporting him while he wrote SATs, letters, resumes and essays. I was available to him virtually 24/7 throughout his last six months of high school. The thought of losing him made me so sad; the sense of loss that engulfed me was way out of proportion. Some nights I'd go into his room and just look at him. He'd laugh and say, "Mom, I'm not going to disappear. Go to bed." He tolerated me with good humour. I'd say, "I don't know how I'll live without you, Hud." He'd laugh. "I told you there's therapy for this problem, Mom. You can get it now, in advance of my departure." It was a standing joke around the house. Mom was going to be an emotional wreck when Hudson left.

In March of his graduating year, he heard from the schools he'd applied to and was offered spots at his top picks. He chose Notre Dame in the U.S. because of its stellar reputation for sports and its academic status as the number one Catholic university in North America. I talked about getting an apartment in Chicago so I'd be close enough for him to visit me on weekends. Needless to say, he did not encourage me.

As summer approached, we got ready for our big ski trip to the Cordillera of the Southern Andes, in Chile—Hudson's graduation present—with Brian and I going on to Las Leñas after Hudson returned home to get ready for Notre Dame. Brian put in long hours at the office in preparation for our departure and appreciated the attention I was devoting to Hudson and Hilary. In the evenings, Brian assembled our equipment and tuned our skis, which he keeps in a room in the basement, and finalized arrangements with our wonderful guide and dear friend, Kees. It was all figured out: Hilary would go off to summer camp and return when Brian and I came home from the Andes, and we would all get into the car for Hudson's trip to Indiana. Upon our return from getting Hudson off to university, I'd go back to my consulting work, totally re-charged and refreshed by another incredible skiing trip to South America. Brian would have completed his holidays and return to his office as President and CEO of NCR Canada. That was the plan.

Having confirmed our dates and Kees' availability, I set out a demanding physical training schedule for myself, to prepare for the grueling 18-day trip. I worked out every day in the off season anyway, to stay in shape for backcountry skiing, but in preparation for a big trip like the Andes I went at it extra hard. At a gym near my house, a trainer who specializes in working with performance athletes put me on an intense program that included circuit training, weights, push-ups, sit-ups, lunges and squats. He had me jumping rope for three minute bursts. (Sounds easy? Try it.) He'd start his sessions saying, "Who's the champ? Who's the champ?" I'd laugh and say, "I'm the champ." He'd say, "You're training like a pro. You're pro level now." I'd say, "Shut up, Craig." A couple of times I burst into tears with the pain. "I can't take it, Craig, you're killing me." I ran, cycled, pumped iron, dieted and held my stretches.

That was in Toronto in May and June 2004. After a month at Whistler with Hilary—I ran up and down the mountain and worked out hard every day—I came home in fighting form, feeling ready for the Andes. On July 27, we dropped Hilary off at a friend's house for a ride to summer camp, and the three of us—Brian, Hudson and I—headed to the airport, our gear packed into the back of the car. We were well outfitted. Each of us had two pairs of skis and poles, skins (Velcro-like strips that adhere to the bottom of skis, for climbing), trekker bindings (enabling the heel of the boot to lift while climbing), extra shells for ski boots, helmets, water bottles, probes and beacons. We carried all the backcountry essentials, the tools to perform an avalanche rescue if required. We each had a metal shovel that could be dismantled for easy packing. Our beacons (or digital avalanche transceivers) showed the distance and direction of buried victims on an easy-to-read display. We had a snap-together metal rod that formed a 12-foot-long probe to poke down into the snow to pinpoint the body after tracking it down with our beacon. Tool kits with wrenches and screwdrivers were important for equipment repair, and first aid kits with bandages and moleskin were key to dealing with blisters and scrapes. As Brian liked to say, "You don't just show up in the backcountry and climb. You have to be prepared with the right gear."

I had two pairs of my favorite Volkl "fat skis," as we called off piste skis, which tend to be a little wider, shorter and heavier than regular skis, weighing more—adding to the weight of the pack as we climbed. They're harder to manoeuvre but they provide more buoyancy in deep snow. Powder can be up to your chest and you'd die of exhaustion trying to move through it without the right equipment.

We had never visited Santiago before so we spent a day touring the Chilean capital, walking the streets, exploring. It's a vibrant city, exciting, bustling with energy. Hip restaurants are plentiful all over the downtown area. Hudson took it all in; we enjoyed watching him absorb the culture, the surroundings. The following day we proceeded to southern Chile for two days of warm-up skiing, before meeting up with Kees. Traveling through the famous Chilean vineyards en route to the mountains was a beautiful drive. The skiing was first rate and we had wonderful accommodations. The powder was so good in-bounds we didn't need to climb off piste.

Following an awesome trip to Termas de Chillan, a really good resort with lots of vertical and the longest runs in South America, we returned to Santiago to meet Kees, an exceptional skier and person. He had provided us with strong leadership in the mountains on many different trips. Our next stop was Portillo, Chile, the most famous and oldest ski centre in South America, about 140 km. from Santiago. Portillo is well known for fine summer snow, good skiable terrain and some of the best remote mountain accommodation anywhere. We were rested, acclimatized and ready to hit the mountains, big time. Kees was fresh off a successful climbing expedition to Mount McKinley (Denali), in Alaska. He and his team were part of a very small and exclusive group to climb and ski the mountain from its summit that year. He was rested and ready to show us some of the best extreme skiing in the world. Hudson was pumped.

Leaving Santiago by car, Brian was behind the wheel. With the music turned up full blast, he drove dangerously fast through a blinding snowstorm, eager for a quicker arrival at Portillo. We belted out the words as Jimmy Hendrix wailed on his guitar and the car barreled along a narrow, twisting road that cut deep into the Andes mountains. It was a frightening trip, our tiny rented car loaded with gear and four full-sized passengers, chains on the tires, grinding up steep inclines with no guard rails, along a series of tight mountain switchbacks that took us higher and higher into the Andes. All of a sudden a dark shape loomed ahead of us, charging at us at full speed. It was a giant snowplow. On a single-lane mountain road. I think we all just closed our eyes and said good night. I don't know how we passed it safely; I swear there were millimeters between our little car and that huge machine.

It was still snowing heavily when we arrived in Portillo, a magical location for a ski area, set beside a mountain lake which added to the romantic feel of the place. But the next day, up on the mountain, I had trouble plowing through the snow. It was very deep, wet and heavy. I felt weak and out of shape. I'd trained like crazy, I should have been stronger than I'd ever been, yet I wasn't skiing well. I fretted about my equipment— last year's Volkl skis. Something wasn't right, yet I'd skied well during our previous trip to the Andes. That was last year, when I was 46. Now I was 47. Hudson had just turned 18. I watched him ski with Brian and Kees and I was filled with a sense of overpowering love. I wasn't really losing him, I kept telling myself, he was growing up; our relationship would deepen over the years. As a mother, I had nothing to worry about. Yet I wasn't on my game. I felt paralyzed, in a way—it was about Hudson, having to let him go, perhaps feeling my own grief about losing my father.

The Portillo area was steep—exactly what we had searched for—but the skiing after a few days became very hard work for me. I finally managed to put in one respectable day but I did not feel I was in top form, despite all the conditioning and preparation I'd done. I felt myself hesitating; I was uncertain and holding back, and my skiing showed it. Brian, Hudson and Kees, on the other hand, had an awesome trip and hiked above the lifts. They skied on top of a volcano. One day after a heavy snowfall there was a point release slide (loose snow avalanche) while they were climbing up. I was below them and saw it. It was an eerie feeling, watching them come close to being in serious trouble. I was frightened. My reaction was exaggerated and very protective. I freaked out at them and forbade them from going back up, which was not like me. They laughed and humoured me. "Come on, Carol, the snow's already fallen. It never falls twice in the same place. Where's your guts?" The sound of the slide rang in my ears for days after.

The frustration I felt with my own skiing, and my heightened sense of alarm, dissipated in the warmth of being with my husband and son in the mountains. It was impossible not to have fun with them. Together we enjoyed sunny days and long lunches at Tio Bob's at the summit. We dined out every night in the formal dining room at the hotel, drank the best Chilean wine, ate scrumptious Argentinian beef, and attempted to show Hudson a good time, exploring the region. I don't recall ever experiencing such fabulous food and hospitality as we did during those evenings at Portillo's beautiful hotel at the base of the mountain. On our final day we were snowed in. The only road leading in and out of Portillo was closed. There had been a huge dump (65cm) of snow and we were forced to stay another night.

Finally escaping Portillo, we drove Hudson to the airport in Santiago and said our goodbyes. He was flying to Miami and then Toronto, going home to pack for university. It was August 8. Brian and I would be back in ten days to take him to school. In the meantime, we would carry on to Argentina, for our second week. I hugged Hudson close. I choked back tears and tried to brush my feelings aside. Plagued by a deep apprehension, a sense of exhaustion, I remembered the dream I'd had when I was 16, before my father died: I was holding a bag of popcorn and the stadium exploded; popcorn whirled around my head as the world came to an end. I tried to shake it off. What was the matter with me? Why was I feeling this despair?

From Santiago, we flew to Buenos Aires and then to Malargue, the gateway to skiing the Andes in the Mendoza province of Argentina. The flight into Malargue took us from sea level to about 3,000 feet and was "a bit of a gong show," as Brian put it. The plane was overloaded with wealthy South Americans and backcountry fanatics and all their gear. The scene at the Malargue airport was frenetic, with passengers trying to find their equipment and fend off local children begging for money. From there, we boarded a bus for a 75-minute ride through desert scrub up into the

Andes. The mountains loomed at us through the windows as the bus went higher, up to 7,200 feet above sea level at the base of Las Leñas.

The next ten days were to be dedicated to skiing Las Leñas, the summer mecca of powder skiing in the steepest part of the Andes. We returned to the same hotel we'd stayed at the previous summer, for our 20th anniversary. Argentina is a very sexy place and Hotel Pisces a flashy resort with a casino, good dining room and hotel accommodation. Plus the best off piste skiing in the summer. Hard-core backcountry skiers didn't usually stay at the Hotel Pisces and there we were with our packs, our technical equipment and our determination to get out of the bar early enough in the evening to catch the first lift in the morning. With a stop to watch the starry skies at night—skies so clear and black, stars so dazzlingly bright, I was reminded of the North.

Upon our arrival, it was obvious the landscape in-bounds was missing the deep snow that had fallen during our previous trip. We thought we needed a big storm before we could get ourselves up to high elevation (14,000 feet) for the steepest and deepest skiing. Definitely feeling let down, we began the patient wait for snow to fall out of the sky. But we were hopeful. Each day we "signed the book," a strict requirement at Las Leñas, detailing our planned departure time and route and when we expected to come back. (If you don't sign the book, you can be banned from Las Leñas.)

Day One, Brian and Kees climbed and I stayed in range. I found the snow to be hard packed and very fast. Rocks were plentiful. The snow conditions were far worse than anticipated, in bounds. We didn't know what was happening in the backcountry. We worried that unless the mother of all storms—the Monte Rosa, which usually appeared in September—arrived early, we were going to be hard pressed to gain access to anything close to the skiing we'd enjoyed off the summit last year, when we'd climbed every day.

Day Two, we were still watching for signs of a storm and praying for the Monte Rosa to arrive. I skied in-bounds and felt satisfied that my skiing was returning to top form. I was much more relaxed. Hudson was safely back home and I was feeling less protective of him and more adventurous. The guys cruised at high, high speeds and checked out a few short climbs but had yet to report a killer run. That evening over a glass of wine at the hotel bar, we talked about going into the backcountry the next day, all three of us. "Yeah, I'm up for it," I said.

CHAPTER SEVEN

The Accident

August 11, 2004

DAY THREE. TIME IS MONEY. Extreme skiing is an expensive sport and up here, at this altitude—12,000 feet at the top of the chairlifts—we were eager to get our money's worth. Brian and I had flown thousands of miles for the most spectacular off piste skiing in the world, and today was the day. The night before, Kees had spoken to a few of his fellow guides and figured out a route that involved a fairly steep climb—though nothing more strenuous than we had completed on a daily basis during the previous year's trip—to get us into decent snow. The idea was to give me a good day of skiing, to regain my confidence in the best snow available. The higher you go in elevation, generally the better the snow is.

We awakened as usual at 6:30 am. The sky was still black, glittering with stars. The sun would not rise for another hour but from our balcony we could see the entire mountain range—awesome, massive shapes looming in the darkness around us, waiting for us. We were looking forward to getting into the backcountry. After a typical mountain breakfast of cereal and eggs, I began to mentally prepare for what lay ahead.

As the sun came up, we could see that it was a bluebird day. Not a cloud in the sky, light winds and no worries about avalanches. Kees had studied the weather patterns and followed the reports extensively. All systems were a go. I was totally comfortable with the route and fully prepared for weather changes. My pack, including my skis, weighed about 50 pounds and was loaded with water, snacks, probes, and shovel. I am not a big person—5'5" tall, 130 pounds—but I was in good condition and accustomed to the exertion. We set off for the day, climbing. Above us we could see a few thousand feet of wide-open terrain—a spectacular sight.

The climb was long but not dangerous or difficult and we were delighted with what we found: lots of snow. It was all good. But I found myself moving slowly; it was hard at times to maintain a good, strong, steady pace. Was I holding the boys back? I had anticipated a one-hour climb from the traverse at the base but it became three hours or more. Occasionally, I stepped into hip-deep powder and buried a leg fully into the snow. Feeling mild fatigue, I continued upwards with my head down trying to maintain a positive frame of mind. After all, it was a banner day to be in the Andes. There was no reason to doubt myself.

About a third of the way up, a young American from Colorado came up behind us. He was very talkative, which I found disruptive. Then along came a guy from Powder King, B.C. who was skinning up the mountain (with skins on the bottom of his skis) and got so hot he stripped off his jacket and shirt. Brian and Kees and I rarely ran into people in the backcountry; the three of us worked as a team, quiet and serious and focused on our efforts.

Off piste skiing is not a game. It's a high risk sport and you have to be super alert at all times. But with all the chitchat on the mountain, I felt I was losing my focus. I was distracted. Three-quarters of the way up, we took a break, rehydrated and assessed the situation. I took a good look down at all the lines. It was a sensational view: steep, untracked powder, virgin snow reaching for miles along the spine of the Andes mountains, so stark and majestic they looked God-like. Exactly what we were searching for. This is going to be an incredible day of skiing, I thought, then sensed a tiny bit of hesitation deep inside my body. I was tired. We were into our second full week of skiing in the Andes and maybe I needed to take a day off. I tried to comfort myself: I'll be good once I get my skis on and start my descent.

Brian looked at me and asked if I wanted to turn back. He wanted me to know he wasn't pushing me beyond my limits. "No," I answered firmly. We three said our good-byes to the "interlopers" and agreed to stick with the plan to climb up to the summit of Cerro Torrecillas. Kees suggested I take the lead for the final ascent. This boosted my confidence. Any time I got the lead over Brian, I always felt good. I am competitive that way.

When we reached the summit, I felt great. We were just under 14,000 feet on top of one of the steepest skiing mountains in the Andes. I had been climbing for over three hours and I had reached the summit first. To top it off Brian and I were with our close friend Kees, a strong and experienced mountaineer, whom I totally trusted. The intensity of the off piste experience forms strong bonds, but Brian and I were not easy clients for Kees. We could pressure him into difficult situations because we were headstrong, we went after what we wanted and we didn't back down.

We rested a few minutes at the summit and drank in the beauty of our surroundings. Man, this was one out-of-the-park, crystal clear, beautiful day. My adrenalin was pumping. I was experiencing that peculiar rush my body gets when it is challenged. Gazing out over the snowcapped peaks that stretched for miles in all directions, I felt like we were on another planet, the only humans privileged to see one of the most magnificent vistas anywhere in the world.

I began assembling my equipment. My pack was loaded and adjusted tightly on my back. Care was taken to ensure my avalanche beacon was safely in place, inside my jacket. I removed the snow from the bottom of my boots and snapped into my skis. As we traversed across a very narrow ridge at the top of the summit, looking for the right line down, I saw that it was going to be trickier than I'd anticipated. This was extreme at its most extreme. I would have to push off from the ridge, an icy wind blown crust of snow (cornice like) that acted like a lip or ledge hanging from the top of the mountain. From the ridge it was a 90 degree vertical drop into the chute, which was insanely steep and no wider than 20 feet, bordered on both sides by jagged rock bands. The chute led straight down into a slightly wider couloir that would drop us further into an even larger bowl where we'd find the best available powder, a long run, the best skiing. Where we would fly.

Brian and Kees assessed the terrain. The drop-off at every section of the ridge was extremely steep. Brian sensed my apprehension and suggested I move back to take one of the easier skiing lines we had passed on the way up. I refused. I pushed forward, insisting on continuing with the planned route. I wanted us to stick together and never once considered turning back, taking a lesser route, going it alone. Not today, not ever, that simply was not me. I didn't want to ruin the day or the run, just because I was feeling sketchy.

Brian asked a second time if I would turn back. "No," I said, silently thinking, *Never. It is not negotiable.* The line was selected. We all knew the drill. Brian was to go first, I would be second and Kees third. The two most trusted individuals on the mountain would encircle me, one in front and the other behind. We were experienced skiers with close to 100 years of combined skiing among us. Yet I felt unaccountably vulnerable and uneasy. Suddenly, I felt very alone.

Brian stood on the edge of the ridge and I lined up behind him, readying my position. Brian paused; I could read his body language. This was a difficult entry even for him. This made me nervous; he's one of the most competent off piste skiers I've ever seen. He pushed off and dropped into a chute so steep and narrow we lost sight of him the instant he left the top.

Brian's cautious entry into the chute was not a good sign for me as I often gained confidence from watching him rip down mountains. This was not the case today. Everything suddenly became weird for me. There was a bizarre feeling in the air. I had noticed Brian bracing himself as he drove his skis straight down, which reinforced my sense of unease. Was I hallucinating? Maybe Brian didn't brace himself. Did he hesitate? My mind was racing. I stared down the chute, bound by rocks on both sides. Once I left the top of the ridge and got into the chute, the turns had to be short-radius because it was so frighteningly narrow. I would have to make six, maybe seven turns of the steepest, most terrifying type I had ever executed.

My thoughts jumped to 11 months earlier when we'd first come to the Andes. I'd ruled. I'd skied better than I'd ever skied in my life. I tried to pump myself up, I tried to tell myself that we'd come out to have fun, to ski in the best snow available, but I could not hold the thought. My mind bounced and ricocheted. I couldn't focus. I looked down the chute and tried to point my skis. There was dead silence. My senses were completely elevated. I heard Brian radio up to Kees, "Take it slow, go easy, it's really steep, there is no room for error." I waited to hear the last of Brian's radio voice and then I pushed off.

The snow was hard packed, boiler plate, the slope thinly covered and icy. It felt like I was on top of the CN Tower, looking straight down, trying to ski down the side of the tower. It was lights out if I slipped, for even a nano-second; it would be impossible to regain my balance. I was fighting with myself now, thinking, *Oh dear God, Brian made it down. He's mentally tough. Smarten up. Grab hold of yourself.*

I'd never, ever skied anything of this magnitude, not anywhere in the Alps, Monashees, Selkirks, Bugaboos, Rockies or Coastals, not anywhere I had been on the planet. *It's unskiable*, I thought, but I had no choice, I was on it. I tried to rip an edge into the slope. I had to get control of my emotions, my mind, my body. The fight was on. There was no time to spare, I was moving into the narrow chute. Before I knew what was happening, I was sliding backwards in space, back-diving and looking straight down the chute. I was airborne. I had fallen off the mountain. There was no stopping me now. The rock faces glared at me as I plummeted toward them and between them. I had no room to manoeuvre. I would have little chance of survival if my body veered off the fall line. The blow of hitting the rocks would kill me instantly. I had miscalculated the dangers that lay ahead.

Everything went into slow motion as I fell at a speed I'd never experienced before, falling hundreds of feet downward. I was aware of Brian below me for an instant and called out, "Please stop my fall, please stop me." I couldn't actually see him on the mountain, but I knew he was there somewhere, watching over me. This gave me tremendous comfort and strength in a morbid kind of way. My mind was racing at a fierce speed searching for survival tactics. My body's natural instinct was to tighten up and curl into a fetal ball to brace myself for the blows that without a doubt would come. Everything was white and very bright. I was aware of the rock cliffs on either side of me but knew nothing of what lay below. I had no idea where I was. I had lost control of my body. Then a powerful voice in my head took over, an impulse formed in my mind: Stay loose. Do not tighten up. If there is any chance of survival, YOU HAVE TO STAY LOOSE. Every cell of my being was wired to this mantra: STAY LOOSE, STAY LOOSE, STAY LOOSE. It repeated over and over in an unstoppable loop. My body responded. It was limp.

The descent was vertical and very rapid. I was free falling, rag dolling, pin wheeling, hurtling and rocketing down the mountain at breakneck speed, back flip over back flip, head to toe, no sign of where I was headed, no longer a person but simply an object out of control. STAY LOOSE.

The first drop-off I remember clearly because I had taken off head first in a backward position, a reverse swan dive. The initial drop was terrifyingly long before I started to hit the mountain. STAY LOOSE. My body picked up speed and with each blow on the mountain I was tossed back up into the air again. The impact of every jolt was shattering. My equipment vanished—gloves, poles, skis, goggles—and with each hit I bounced off again, flying 20 feet up in the air, catapulting down the mountain at the speed of terminal velocity. It was over 2,000 vertical feet of non-stop falling, cartwheeling, pin wheeling and rag dolling, fully conscious.

After the first major blow my body took from the mountain, I thought, I AM ALIVE. It's working, STAY LOOSE. I remember every blow. The fall seemed endless, a nightmare without end. It carried me down through the narrowest of chutes, around a rock cut, and straight down the entire face of the mountain. An incredible distance along terrifyingly rugged terrain with jagged rocks and dangerous drop-offs.

My body and mind became detached from one another. I had brief flashes of my mother and my children. I saw Hudson's face, and Hilary's. I was in another world, sailing off the mountain into the void and then crashing into the mountain over and over again.

Suddenly my body stopped. Silence, no sign of further crashing. My mind took a few moments to re-connect. I AM ALIVE. My eyes opened. It was a beautiful, sunny day. A bluebird day. I had no idea where I was. I had survived the worst catastrophe on the mountain. I AM ALIVE! The triumph made me high. Wow. I looked out over the valley and my heart sank. Maybe this is heaven. Maybe I'm dead. But no, I could see something moving in the distance.

I don't know how long it took before my brain registered PAIN. Body, arms, legs—I felt like I had been shattered into a million pieces, raging pain in every cell of my body, knifing into my neck, then my back and all the way down my left side. I was paralyzed! Oh my God. No, I was not! I moved my head slightly and my right hand could clench a fist, the left hand could not.

The brightness of the sun shining down on me was incredibly powerful and uplifting, the warmth like a blessing. I wanted to move. But I was going into shock. I was confused. My body felt frozen with the cold. Frostbite? From a distant place I remembered my mother's warnings about the horrors of frostbite, how she'd made me wear a heavy raccoon coat to walk to skating lessons at six in the morning. Fear of frostbite caught my attention, made me focus. I was terrified of amputation. I had to get myself out of here, wherever I was, right now. A surge of energy—it was the North coming back again.

After what seemed like a long time, Brian arrived. He had witnessed most of the accident, at least the portion that occurred below him. He'd quickly radioed Kees about my location before skiing down to where I lay motionless. Brian remained calm outwardly, but he was shaken to the core. He had witnessed the most staggering crash he had ever seen. The victim was his wife and best friend and the mother of his two children. When he saw me move, he couldn't believe it.

Kees came down as quickly as he could, being careful not to have an accident himself. He collected as much of my gear as he could—as a matter of routine, part of his safety training. My skis and poles were scattered across the lower face of Cerro Torrecillas, and if he hadn't found them, I don't know what would have become of me. My pack was still firmly tied to my back, which no doubt saved my spine. Even so, the pain I felt was unbearable. I was moving into living hell. My neck was numb. My left side was gone from the waist up. I was in serious trouble. I had no feeling in my left arm whatsoever. My shoulder was sticking out the front of my jacket.

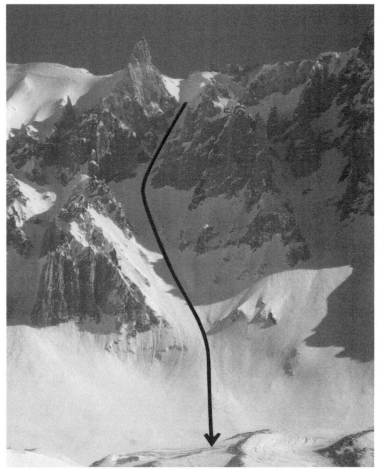

The Fall Line

From a distance—as if they were far away, though they were hovering over me—I heard Brian and Kees talk about rescue options. It was late in the afternoon. One of them would have to ski out to get help. If I waited for help it might not come that night, I thought, and I'd freeze to death. I had to get myself to the hospital immediately. I was fighting unconsciousness; traumatic shock was threatening to take over but my mind was incredibly strong. I fought to stay awake, to regain command of myself. My mind searched for a survival strategy. I concentrated on the details of what I had to do to survive. I had to stand up and get myself out of there. No time to hesitate. I realized where I was—a few miles from the village and the way out required me to traverse, with some moderate downhill skiing, through a series of valleys. I had gone out this way last year and felt I could make it. There was no arguing with me.

Brian and Kees helped me stand up and I motioned for them to remove my pack from my back. I screeched with pain. They could see that my left shoulder was completely dislocated and they were afraid to touch me because they didn't want to make my injuries any worse. They tried to persuade me to wait for help. I didn't look as if I was in any condition to get out on my own but I said, "No. Give me my skis." Miraculously, they had found most of my gear. Brian put my skis on for me. I moved forward. I thought: I am fit to ski. I can move my legs and I have feeling from the waist down. I held a pole in my right hand. My left arm hung lifeless, useless, with my left shoulder totally dislocated as if I were deformed. I was bent over, crippled with pain.

Once I had made up my mind to go there was no stopping me. As I moved slowly down the valley, I heard someone screaming in pain. I didn't know where the sound was coming from at first, then had the shocking realization that the primal roar of agony was coming out of me. The louder I screamed the more the noise seemed to block out the pain that raged through my upper body. Brian and Kees followed behind me in abject silence, riddled with doubt and fear about my course of action, wishing they could do something for me. But with all my years in the mountains and the first-hand knowledge I'd gained at Lake Louise, I knew I had to get out. I was afraid it would take forever for a helicopter to find me. I was sure I would not survive in the backcountry overnight—that's what propelled me forward.

The stabbing, knifing pain had turned me into an animal. I was in my very own hell. All I could think about was survival. About ten minutes into the descent, the excruciating pain made me want to vomit, but I had nothing inside to throw up. I was not sure I could go any further. I stopped moving. I must have had the pathetic look of an injured animal limping along in the forest. Kees put a couple of Tylenol 3s in my mouth and flushed them down my throat with water. He and Brian tried to put my left shoulder back in by tying bandages around my chest in opposite directions and pulling with all their might. After a few minutes of trying and plenty of screaming, they quit. Kees said he'd try again in half an hour, when the painkillers had kicked in.

Skiing forward slowly, I continued howling. The fire in my upper body was beyond comprehension but never did I doubt the possibility of reaching my goal. My phobic concern for frostbite was paramount. I thought the numbness in my left arm was a sign that the limb was freezing. I remembered a guy who'd been helicopter skiing in the Rockies many years ago and the chopper crashed and he couldn't get out of the mountains. He got frostbite and his legs had to be amputated. I did not want to lose my left arm. I had survived this horrific crash and I was determined to keep moving, to save my arm.

Twenty minutes later, Kees tried again. He wrapped bandages in opposite directions across my chest and under both arms. Brian pulled with all his strength on one side and Kees on the other. This was their last shot and they really went for it, gave it all they had. The look of terror in my eyes must have horrified them. I moaned to drown out the pain. I thought I would break in half down the center of my body, but the force at which I was pulled apart allowed my shoulder to slide back into place. It was a new kind of hell. I don't remember feeling any relief when the shoulder slid back into the socket. Kees examined me and confirmed that it was back in place. I was still in so much pain, I didn't believe him. But if they hadn't forced the shoulder back in, I would have lost consciousness.

There was no time to waste. As the pain intensified, I pressed on, skiing faster as we got closer to the base village, startling Brian and Kees with my speed. Preserving every miniscule bit of energy I could muster, I stayed strong and steady throughout the remainder of the run-out. The whole return back to the clinic probably took two and a half hours—of brutal, gut wrenching pain. Thank god I'd trained so hard before heading to South America; my strong legs got me out of the valley that day. Without those quads, without those runs up and down the mountain at Whistler, I never would have made it.

Arriving at the base I was met by ski patrollers at the hut who had heard about the accident. In high hazard areas, they scan through binoculars and telescopes from time to time, to see who's up there. The patroller who'd seen me fall from the summit had assumed the worst and sent out the word: Death on the mountain. He hadn't spotted me moving at the bottom, and there was no time to explain. I was immediately transferred to the Swiss Medical Centre, a rudimentary clinic five minutes down the road from the patrol hut. Two wonderful medical doctors, a traumatologist and a family practitioner, took over. They had been informed about the accident and were prepared to treat me for shock and hypothermia. They were careful not to move me for fear of severe neck and head injuries. Eventually they x-rayed me as best they could with the facilities they had on site, and determined that—much to their astonishment—I had no broken bones, apart from what they thought were some broken ribs. (I was having trouble breathing.) But they didn't have any MRI equipment and they were concerned about the swelling and fluid buildup from all my injuries. They were certain the shoulder was back in place and felt that the best course of action was for me to return to Toronto and get treated there. This was not an overnight hospital. They taped me up, prescribed trauma medication for both shock and injuries, drove me back to the hotel and told me to rest and remain still. "You are one lucky woman to be alive," I was told. Their faces reflected amazement. They called me "a walking miracle." They couldn't believe I'd skied out. As long as I live, I will be eternally grateful to them for caring for me and helping me take the first steps toward healing.

With the doctors promising to stay on-call in case I needed them, armed with mega painkillers and my left shoulder taped up, I was taken to the hotel for bedrest. I was in the twilight zone, a total zombie, but somehow I convinced the people closest to me that I was doing pretty well, considering. It was a massive fraud, perpetrated for the "best reasons." We were scheduled to stay another week, but Brian wanted us to go home the next day. "No," I said, "you and Kees must finish off the trip and we'll all go home together." I needed some time to prepare to face my children. I didn't want them to see me like this, and I was in too much pain to travel. In truth, I was in such deep shock—as was Brian—that I was unable to do anything. I was unraveling, and didn't want to fall apart on the plane or at home. In the distorted logic of trauma, I felt that "hiding out" in Las Leñas was the best option, for the moment. Maybe this horror hadn't really happened.

It's hard to explain my reactions and responses during this time. Neither Brian nor I knew anything about trauma. Brian and I kept talk of the accident to a minimum—which was our style. In the past, if he or Hudson had crashed on a mountain, they'd downplay the incident. It was part of the scene of extreme skiing. No crybabies allowed. It was mostly a male world, and men pride themselves on being tough, not showing weakness. I knew how to do that. Brian told me briefly that while he was standing on the mountain watching my body rocketing through the air, racing toward him, he had moved into the path to attempt to block me. He saw me fly right over his head, 20 feet above him, moving at 80 miles an hour, he estimated. He described the sensation as standing on the side of a highway and seeing a bus fly past at full speed. Had our bodies ever connected at the force with which I was falling, he said, we surely both would have been killed instantly.

I couldn't sleep that night, or for many nights to come. When I closed my eyes, I was engulfed in the nightmare—the playback of the fall, over and over and over again. I couldn't get it to stop. Every time I thought I was sleeping, I'd be falling. I existed in a state of mute terror, unable to say what I was feeling and seeing, for much of the week—indeed, for many months to come. The accident silenced me for a long, long time. Brian had nightmares too, but didn't tell me until much later. He was totally conflicted: thrilled I was alive, petrified by the fragile state I was in. "You were like a drowning victim who's been resuscitated and dies from shock—that's how tenuous your hold was on life."

> *Brian Sullivan: "In a weird way we were happy and celebrating. Carol had survived the accident. It didn't kill her. Next to death, that looked pretty good. But we were in shock and we didn't know what she was going through. The next day, she insisted Kees and I go skiing. I didn't want to leave her alone but she said she'd be fine. Kees and I climbed Sans Salida, which means "no exit." When we looked over the edge and saw that it was 800 feet straight down, we decided to get the hell out of there. It was a bad choice. We had to use an ice pick to get out. The toughest thing is to know when to turn back."*

I was on automatic pilot for the rest of the week in Las Leñas. I lay flat in bed, icing my neck, and spent most of the day in and out of tears. I tried to join Brian and Kees for meals but I wasn't hungry and I wasn't good company. I was in so much pain I could barely eat or talk. It was hard to fake it but I felt I had to "put on a good face" for them—typical "performance behaviour" from my childhood. You had to be tough. No time for bellyaching. On one level, Brian bought it. I told him I was being well looked after by the doctors and he could see for himself that I was able to get up and walk around, albeit like a zombie. He was dancing around on eggshells, trying to help me, trying to figure out what was happening to me, while I was locked in a state of numbness, trying to pretend I was okay. I was desperate to have time alone to try to come to terms with my accident. I demanded that Kees and Brian go off skiing.

Mary Armstrong, trauma therapist: "Carol's wounds weren't visible. She looked like herself. If she'd had casts on both arms and legs, people would have reacted differently, they would have known she'd been badly hurt. But she looked so good—and she is a tough cookie. She is a strong, brave woman and she presented herself as whole, though in reality she was torn apart. But that was her style, to never show 'weakness.' To laugh it off. And of course, her husband wanted her 'back to normal,' wanted to believe she was okay."

I was better off alone. In that silent period, I felt terribly guilty about the accident and what could have been my death, which would have caused an enormous tragedy for my husband and children—similar to the loss created by my father's untimely death when I was 18. How could I have risked my life when Hilary was only 9 years old and Hudson had just turned 18? What would my children's lives be like without a mother? I lay there quietly weeping while the boys were out skiing. When they returned for dinner, I got out of bed and walked slowly to the dining room. I felt as if everyone was staring at me, as if I were a freak. Every skier in the region had heard about the crash, but nobody dared approach me. I wasn't talking. I was in shock and pain and loaded with painkillers, barely able to think. But somehow, I put on a good show—so good that I "got back on the mountain." Which shows how delusional we all were.

On our last day, all taped up, in a sling, I got on the chairlift. At the top, I was frozen in the chair but Brian and

Kees coaxed me off. They escorted me to the Santa Fe hut for lunch. Then I thought I could ski down. I desperately wanted to prove I could return to the mountain. (As a child I had a terrible riding accident; the horse shied approaching a culvert with water in it and I fell off and landed on my head. I was delirious, but one of my brothers picked me up and made me get back on the horse. I ended up in the hospital with a severe concussion.)

They put my skis on for me. I snowplowed down a bunny hill, more like crawled down, I can't really describe it as skiing because I was so heavily medicated. I didn't know what I was doing and it was a stupid thing to do—illuminating the nature of profound trauma. None of us understood how damaged I was. I was wasted and I was faking "normalcy," which I did pretty well. I'd never known such vulnerability in my life, such discord between my exterior image and inner self.

When the skis were removed at the base of the mountain that day, I told them, "That's the last time I'll ever ski." I was trapped inside a body that was a wreck, mentally and physically. Nobody knew how I felt. I was really angry with myself. I was afraid I'd be ruined forever. How could I face my children? How could I let them know I'd been so stupid, I'd nearly died, I'd nearly deprived them of their mother? The emotional and mental trauma I would suffer had only just begun. I didn't know it, but I was a changed person, never to return to my old self again.

"The definition of trauma: an experience that is intolerable and inescapable for the human brain. You can't run from it, can't fight it, can't flee from it. No superhuman power can deal with it. Your body's survival mechanism is to let the body freeze and become numb." *Mary Armstrong, trauma therapist.*

CHAPTER EIGHT

Recovery & Rehab

August 12, 2004 to March, 2006

AS WE PACKED UP TO leave Las Leñas, I couldn't feel anything. I could have put my hand on a hot stove and not felt the skin burn. That was nerve damage. It was physical. I had this other numbness, the automatic pilot, the denial. It was mental numbness. I couldn't talk about the accident and seemed clueless about what was going on around me.

Pain is a weird thing. It can take over your entire being, but nobody can see it; you can't adequately describe it and if you try, you feel like you're complaining. I didn't want to be a whiner or a downer. So I had nothing to say. In the days after the accident leading to our flight home to Toronto, I was in a haze, a form of shocked silence. All I could think about was, What am I going to tell my children?

On the way home, we had a stopover in Buenos Aires. With no plans for the evening, we all decided to go to "Señor Tango," a famous show about the history and meaning of the Argentinian dance that is at the root of gaucho culture. I insisted on going with them, as strange as it sounds. I was doing a pretty good job convincing them that I was recovering. There are photographs of me smiling, red lipstick in place, seated at a table in the Senor Tango club. I look normal. These images demonstrate an old truth, that you can't always believe your eyes. Brian and Kees loved the show. I was in so much pain and groggy from painkillers that I can't remember the evening. Looking back, I am astonished by the force of the invisible hand of trauma and how it seals its victims in a tomb. It's not that my husband and Kees were uncaring; it's that I was hiding the pain and didn't know how to do anything else.

Brian: "My nightmares continued for months, but I didn't tell her. I kept seeing her falling from the mountain, her face up in the air as she flew over me, the terror in her eyes. I'd wake up, sweating. I felt guilty."

The next day we flew to Santiago and then on to Toronto. The flight was exhausting. We were in the air for more than fifteen hours and there was so much turbulence I began to feel paralysis in areas of my body that had full movement before the plane took off. I was wearing a soft support roll around my neck and just sat there, more or less immobilized, in horrific pain. Brian tried to look after me but there was not much he could do apart from trying to pour water and painkillers down my throat. And make me understand what he was saying: everything was going to be OK; he was going to resign as President and CEO of NCR Canada and take care of me. I was so out of it I didn't realize the significance of his decision.

The severity of my accident kicked in as soon as I got home and saw my children. The reality hit that I would probably never run, skate or ski with them again. For a family in which sports was the glue that held us together, this was a devastating prospect. I envisioned myself disabled for the rest of my life. I felt hopeless. Every time I closed my eyes I saw myself falling off the mountain. I had not slept in a week.

I was still incapable of talking about what had happened to me to anyone. It terrified me to think about the accident. I had no words for it. It was an awful burden that isolated me from everyone around me, but I thought that if I didn't talk about it and was lucky enough to recover, then I could forget it ever happened. Which was my fervent, hopeless wish: to have the accident expunged, eradicated from my brain. And so I downplayed the extent of my pain and hid my worries about my numbness. I tried to shield Hudson and Hilary and show them how excited I was about the drive to Indiana. Hudson was packed and ready to go. Hilary couldn't wait to see her big brother embark on life at university, giving her a taste of what lay ahead for her in another six or seven years. I really wanted to be part of it.

Hilary, age 9: "When Mom came back from the Andes, I knew she was trying to be strong and act normal but it was scary to look at her. I've hardly ever seen her sick, not even a cold, and I could tell she was suffering. I could see she was in pain. I felt sensitive to her pain. I do every sport you can think of, but I'm a scaredy-cat when it comes to danger."

Hudson, age 18: "I'm insensitive—I'm a guy—but I knew Mom wasn't the same. I guess I didn't really want to know how bad it was. I've been in a fall on a mountain so I know what it's like to lose control and have no ability to stop yourself. It's extremely frightening. But I've never been hurt the way she was. She did her best to hide it, but she couldn't. I mean, she almost died."

I still had no feeling in my left arm and my upper body was numb. My backpack had probably saved my life, but it had jammed up against my neck with each blow to the mountain as I fell. I felt as if the vertebrae in my neck had been dislodged. Was anything broken? My sister Susan had made an appointment for me with the sports medicine specialist Dr. Michael Clarfield. He runs the largest clinic of its kind in Canada and his team is famous for their work with high performance and professional athletes. I saw him at 7:30 on the morning of August 18, 2004, less than 24 hours after I arrived in Canada and seven days after the accident. I had to tell him what had happened to me, but Brian was in the examination room with me, so I was reluctant to admit to the severity of the pain and the lack of feeling—which would be admitting defeat, and would maybe make my prognosis worse. That sounds crazy, but that's what I thought: speaking the injuries could make them permanent. And then I would give up. Damaged goods. Why bother? Every once in a while I thought, Maybe it would have been better if I'd bitten the dust, then my family wouldn't have to go through all this. I didn't know it, but I was exhibiting typical symptoms and responses of someone who had experienced severe trauma.

Still more or less in shock and jet-lagged from the return flight, I recounted the story of the fall for the first time in Dr. Clarfield's office. Even then, I pulled back from the worst of it, simply couldn't speak it in front of Brian. Dr. Clarfield examined me, took X-rays and an ultrasound of the left shoulder and neck. I explained that we were leaving for Indiana the same day and he promised to call my cell phone with results while we were en route with Hudson and Hilary.

In the car, I wore a neck brace and a sling and took plenty of painkillers and anti-inflammatories to survive the eight-hour drive. Like my father before me, I lay flat out with the seat fully reclined, a step away from the coffin. But I had to be there, absolutely could not have endured missing out on Hudson's launch at university. It felt like all the pent-up years of mothering my son, all the work and nurturing and love and devotion were culminating in his departure. I would have died rather than stay home. Call me headstrong. Brian knew there was no arguing with me.

As promised, Dr. Clarfield called before we reached Notre Dame. He had examined the X-rays. I had fractured ribs on the left side and minor vertebrae damage, possibly dislodged but nothing we could not fix. There was so much soft tissue damage and fluid buildup he couldn't tell what was causing all the problems. He wanted me to have MRIs on my neck, spine and head upon my return but the preliminary X-rays looked good. His words gave me great relief. Maybe I wasn't doomed after all.

Saying good-bye to Hudson at Notre Dame was very tough and the pain I was in did not make it any easier. I was broken-hearted; he was in great spirits. We met the other guys who'd be sharing his dorm, and their parents, and I tried to act like a normal woman though I'm sure they thought I was strange. I hung around longer than Hudson wanted me to, and finally he said, "It's time for you to go, Mom, I've got things to do." I cried my eyes out all the way back to the US/Canada border. God Bless Brian and Hilary for putting up with me. The emotional and physical pain of so many things all at once tumbled about inside, knocking me helpless. I was in my weakest state ever, as frail as I'd remembered my father before his death.

Dr. Clarfield saw me back in Toronto the next morning, August 21, ordered MRIs and I began rehab with one of his physiotherapists, Susan Deacon. Sue has two undergraduate degrees—one in kinesiology and a B.Sc in physiotherapy—plus a clinical Masters that she completed in Australia in 2003. She works with athletes ranging from the elite performance level to "weekend warriors," as she puts it.

Without Sue, I'd still be a wreck. That first day, I had zero range of motion in my neck, my left arm, and my shoulder. But my denial was so deep that I thought I'd see her every day for a few weeks, and somehow I'd get better, back to normal, back to my life. Two years later, I'm still dealing with the extent of the damage. Sue's greatest gift to me, apart from her expertise, was to teach me patience with my body. Patience was not one of my virtues. Vulnerability frightened me. Would I ever get strong again? I didn't know it, but I was embarking on a journey that would take me to places as challenging as off piste skiing in the Andes. I would have to learn to feel compassion for myself. It's true what they say: wisdom can come from suffering if you walk through it, step by step, day by day. In my case, baby steps. Tiny chin tucks. One-inch head nods. The hardest things I've ever done.

In the first three weeks, Sue got me to do tiny chin tucks, ten at a time, and rest, over and over again. That's all I could do, and every move was painful—which scared me. Riddled with tension and fear, I couldn't shut off the adrenalin. I had an obnoxious, Triple A personality attitude (so ignorant, so frightened was I): I'm going to see Sue every day and I'm going to fix this thing in three weeks. Yeah, sure. I was lying on the floor with her and couldn't lift my arm. All I could do was a chin tuck. A goddam chin tuck! She'd put me in traction—with clamps on my head, and she'd pull on my spine to try to stretch it out—and I'd be sobbing. I couldn't take the confinement of traction. I was a mess but I didn't really understand how badly I was injured. Yet everything she told me to do, I did precisely. "Bring it on," I said. Such bravado. But it helped. I was like a little kid again, trying to climb the tower with my older brothers.

The process of getting my neck to move was slow and painful. By November 8, I was able to do one-inch head nods. The one-inch nods were so gentle they almost made me crazy. I couldn't do anything with force. Imagine a performance athlete after two months of rehab having to rest after doing one-inch head nods, ten times. I'd come out of these sessions feeling, I'm never going to get through this, this is going to take forever. I'd never been seriously injured before and the fear of permanent disability haunted me. As did the meaning of "accident." I was obsessed about how, when you're skiing in the backcountry, you're having a great time and you don't think, What if I have an accident? When the accident occurs, you feel like a fool. What kind of idiot was I to get in such a stupid accident? Every accident is stupid, because it means you've made a mistake, and I was brought up to avoid mistakes at all costs. Why couldn't I see it coming? But that's the nature of accidents. They're caused by human error, but we don't see the mistake before we make it. That's the vulnerability of the human condition. No one is perfect. And I, Ms. Perfectionist, had to come to terms with it. I had to learn to let go.

Physically, I was most worried about the loss of feeling in my left arm, which was taped up for a few weeks, then in a sling for another few weeks, then it just hung there. I couldn't lift it up off the table. I couldn't dress myself. After I got the chin tucks and the head nods going, I progressed to arm raises. Lying on the floor on my back, I'd slowly raise my left arm two inches off the floor. That's all I could do. Then I'd rest, relax. Then lift the arm again. And again and again. I would do this all day. If I didn't have an appointment with Sue, I'd go to my gym at home, on the third floor, and do arm raises and chin tucks and head nods for three hours, two sets of 10 repetitions with one to two-minute breaks in between. The pain, just doing such simple little exercises, was excruciating. When I was finished, I'd be exhausted. Yet by the time I'd see Sue for our next session, she'd notice progress. She was very encouraging.

Before Christmas, with a two-pound weight in my left hand, I could lift the arm up perpendicular to the floor, at a 90 degree angle—a spectacular improvement that Sue and I celebrated joyfully. That was the beauty of rehab: you could track your progress and see yourself gaining strength. It was like training for Argentina all over again, except from a different vantage point. This was an important lesson: learning to appreciate my own growth, from where I was. But it was hard; it meant gradually giving up the image (and reality) of myself as super-jock.

If rehab is the active side of recovery, medication is the passive side. I was on painkillers and anti-inflammatories, which no doubt helped me through the worst period, post-accident. Percodan had been prescribed—it's a potent and potentially addictive painkiller. Taking Percodan was what I imagine shooting up with heroin might be like. I felt like I was in a psychedelic movie. Everything was colourful and swirling and whirling. I was tripping out. I couldn't sleep. I was scared of the drug. I thought it—and everything else I was taking— was making me crazy. So I decided to drop the painkillers, cold turkey. I thought: I'm better to feel the pain than to mask it with the crazy feeling of being on drugs. The doctors had wanted me to mask the pain so I could begin the healing process. Well, I was on the path. Now I wanted to get off the drugs, feel the pain and make progress. I was a difficult patient. But I wanted to reconnect with my body. How could I do that if I couldn't feel what it—I—was feeling? Recovery, I discovered, is very much about letting yourself feel again. When what you feel isn't pleasant, it's a tough choice, a huge effort—but I'd been raised to never run away from effort.

A month after the accident, the tremor started. I was sitting in the library at home. I said to Brian, "Why is the house moving?" I was thinking: we have an old house, there's construction outside, or maybe there's an underground quake, although Toronto was a very unlikely earthquake zone.

Brian rolled his eyes as if I was crazy. "The house is not moving, Carol," he said.

"It must be," I said, "because I'm shaking."

"You can't be shaking." He came over and looked closely at me. The shaking started in my legs and progressed to my arms and my lips. It horrified me. I could hide the pain but I couldn't conceal the tremors. From that day on, they came and went of their own volition, appearing without notice any time, anywhere, from a quiet breakfast at home to family parties and public events. I went to see Dr. Clarfield and two neurologists but the shaking mystified them.

I booked myself in for a hair-colouring at Paul King's salon, where I've been going for 20 years. It was a place I totally trusted. I knew I would feel some discomfort but I needed to get my roots done. (I still wanted to look good; that was a good sign.) The new assistant apologized for running hot water down my back while she was trying to cradle my head for support, but I didn't feel a thing. When I took off the robe, it was soaking wet. This really bothered me. I hadn't felt any hot water running down my neck or back. Of course, I couldn't feel the water on my neck or back when I stood in the shower, but at least I had feeling in the rest of my body. Here in the salon, the severity of my numbness and nerve damage suddenly seemed so real, so graphic, and I shed tears that day. This kind of incident set me back, but also gave me a window into my injuries, enabling me to see the long road to recovery ahead of me.

Daily visits to Sue lasted one hour and gradually tapered off to three appointments a week as I worked toward performing the exercises every day at home. She helped show me the extent of my injuries in a gentle way, and spent a lot of time talking to me about what it was going to take to reduce my pain. I could not understand why after six weeks of steady work—like a full time job—I was not seeing major progress. I was still barely able to function. The nightmares continued. I wasn't sleeping. These were difficult times for me and for all the members of my family. I could not hold my head up or stand for more than five minutes at a time. I was unable to drive a car, attend a movie or read a newspaper. I was rendered useless. Yet I had to look after Hilary as best I could and tried to pretend I was getting better. I'd go to her school for a function. People would say, "How was your summer?" I'd be standing with my back against the wall to keep my head propped up straight, and I'd say, "Oh, I had a little accident skiing in the Andes, but I'm going to be okay. I'm in rehab. I'm really lucky." I'd go home and put the neck brace on and lie down to rest and flip through the cycle of nightmares. People would say, "She's doing great, she looks fabulous." I was in living hell. Only Sue knew.

Sue Deacon: "Carol is an elite athlete. I don't have many clients, male or female, who do what Carol does. Backcountry skiers tend to be 'boys,' daredevils. It's a high risk sport for the young, the strong and the fearless. The people who do extreme sports tend to have a very confident manner. You have to have unwavering motivation and determination to succeed. You have to believe you can do anything, you have to be over-confident, almost arrogant—otherwise you'd be afraid. Of course, I met Carol at a time when she was at her most vulnerable. She was all bound up through the neck and shoulders. She started to get tremors during the course of treatment and the tremors alarmed her, understandably, because they could have meant neurological damage, but that hasn't shown up in tests.

After a traumatic injury, the muscles tighten up, to try to protect the wounded joint. The muscles around Carol's neck had gone into a firm spasm that wouldn't let go. I encouraged her to start moving gently, and she did a tremendous amount of work loosening up the joints and muscles. It's completely normal for people to be afraid to let go and relax after trauma; they're afraid they're going to re-injure themselves, so they're holding, they're guarding.

At the beginning, Carol thought she'd be back to normal in no time. She was very motivated and worked very hard. She was over-zealous and had to learn that the healing process was much slower than she wanted. I taught her to respect the healing time. Pain subsiding doesn't mean that tissues have healed. The work has just begun. The healing process is very up and down. Minor setbacks can have a huge mental impact, you can feel you're back to square one. Some people just give up. No matter how tough it was for her, Carol kept going, she pushed through it, time after time. Recovery is never smooth sailing. The mood swings can be difficult to cope with—feeling very upset one minute, then giddy the next, almost manic. People who've experienced traumatic accidents can have trouble controlling their emotions, which is completely normal. Carol escaped something horrendous, but she still had the memory of the accident to deal with. She went through a near-death experience. She was very fortunate, given the nature of what happened, to come out as well as she did.

What astounded me was Carol's determination to get back to skiing in dangerous conditions. I couldn't understand why she was so eager to return to the backcountry—but on the other hand, I see that quite frequently: the more serious the injury, the greater the determination to keep on doing whatever it was they were doing, even if it nearly killed them."

At some crazy level, it gave me strength to return to the backcountry—or at least to believe that I could. It would have been like admitting defeat, to not go back. My love of the mountains helped me formulate a plan. I set rehab goals for myself, outside of physiotherapy: One, to be strong enough at Canadian Thanksgiving in October—two months after the accident—to get in the car with Brian and drive to Notre Dame to see Hudson. Brian would have to do all the driving; I couldn't—the severity of the soft tissue damage, the fluid and swelling, were getting worse and there was nothing more I could do. I was still getting MRIs in attempts to more fully diagnose the damage. Mentally I wasn't great, but I made it to Indiana, and was able to sit through a Notre Dame-Stanford football game in the legendary ND Stadium. Hudson had adjusted well, made a lot of new friends and seemed to be enjoying his first term. He was flourishing. This cheered me up.

Two, to be able to get on a plane the day after Christmas and fly with Brian and the children to Geneva and then to Chamonix, part of a two-month sabbatical we'd decided to take. Three, to get back on skis during that period. "We needed to take the time to recover and get our nerve back," Brian said, and I agreed.

My personal medical journal is full of entries, starting on August 12 and leading up to our post-Christmas departure. On November 25, 2004, I had nerve conduction tests at St. Michael's Hospital. On Dec. 2, I saw my family doctor, Ruth Brooks, at Women's College Hospital, to talk to her about the tremors. She took the time to explain the nature of trauma and suggested I think about writing a book about the accident. I dismissed her idea; what was there to say? I still wasn't talking about it. By December 20, I had the results of three MRI scans of my shoulder, neck and head. One of the neurologists said the nerves were repairing well and there were no lesions to my brain. (At that point, I was happy they'd found a brain.)

Another one said, "Dying isn't the worst thing that could have happened to you on the mountain." What did he mean? That I could have been completely paralyzed, a vegetable on life-support? I didn't stop to ask him. I got my coat and left.

For Brian and I, our lives changed dramatically after the accident. Having given up his CEO position at NCR Canada, he was home with me a lot, supporting me in every way he could (and working on other potential business deals). He drove me to MRI appointments and sat with me in waiting rooms and talked to doctors about what they were seeing. I'd stumble out of appointments with specialists and he'd tell me what they said as he drove me home. I was spending four hours a day at the gym working on every muscle that had been torn and ripped during the accident. I did not return to my job as a marketing consultant. I did not participate in volunteer work at school or in the community. I cancelled our annual Christmas party to benefit Sick Kids Hospital. I attended very few social functions during my recovery. I physically trained and trained and trained. It was as if the North rose up in me—the sense of survival against all odds, the never give up, anything is possible spirit that my father had exemplified. I was infused with his energy. I became obsessed with my progress and tracked it the way an analyst studies statistics. I faced the pain and the facts about my injuries. The fear of being robbed of my ability to enjoy my family and our life in the mountains, drove me forward. I'd felt robbed when I'd lost my father; I was not going to be robbed again.

Slowly, over time, I turned inside out. The woman who ran up and down mountains and had the guts to do extreme skiing discovered that it took more courage to engage in her own recovery—and to do a thousand one-inch head nods—than anything she'd ever done on any mountain anywhere in the world. It was a startling lesson. The Dalai Lama in his book The Art of Happiness says that effort is the final factor in bringing about change. Effort was certainly the major factor in my recovery. I clocked close to two thousand hours in rehab and medical offices and working on my own between September and December 2004, to make a small degree of progress.

The easy way is to give up, but in fact it's harder in the long run because the suffering never ends, and it can get worse. Sharon Salzberg writes, in her essay "Awakening Confidence in Our Own Capacity," that in Western culture, "effort seems burdensome, or even terrifying." Many people think, "I can't do it, I don't have what it takes" to bring about change, she says. "Because we tend to think this way, it is so important to understand what having confidence in ourselves means." She underlines the importance of motivation, commitment, "the willingness to be open," to carry on. "There's no magic to it," she says. And she's right. It means getting up every day, no matter how broken down, and doing it, whatever it is, to take one step forward, to do a one-inch head nod.

On the social circuit before Christmas, 2004, at the holiday parties, I presented myself well. I told people we were going skiing in Europe after Christmas, and they assumed I was fine. Meanwhile, I'd just come from three hours of rehab and wasn't feeling so good. One of the reasons I didn't talk about what I was going through was that I didn't want advice. I wasn't looking for other people's opinions. I felt I was doing everything I possibly could to heal. I had a laser focus. And I didn't want to draw attention to the tremors, which were quite frequent and totally unpredictable. But slowly, as Sue

Deacon had promised, I began to notice progress. I was getting stronger. The numbness was diminishing. I was feeling more like myself.

By the time Hudson came home from Notre Dame in December, I was ready to join the family on an outing to the Ramsden Park rink. Brian, Hudson and Hilary played hockey, and I tried skating—the first physical thing I attempted outside the protection of a gym. But the ice wasn't smooth, my skate got caught in a hole and I took a little tumble. I hurt my shoulder—and had a major setback. The tremor elevated, out of control. I was literally all shook up, unable to stop the trembling. Was it an expression of the terror imprinted in every cell of my body, or was it a sign of healing, of damaged nerves coming back to life? Fears started to surface, especially fear of falling. When we had our first big snowfall, I was terrified walking to the car. I could not step outside my front door without being afraid of falling. Was I crazy to think I could go to the Alps and start skiing again?

On Boxing Day, December 26, 2004, we all flew to Geneva—my first flight since the accident. I was so happy to have the love and comfort of my family around me as we set off on sabbatical for two months. We spent the first ten days at Chamonix in the French Alps. Brian took Hudson and Hilary on the bus every morning to go skiing while I walked around the village, went out for lunch, made dinner reservations, firmed up our itinerary—but didn't ski. They understood I was going through a process of getting comfortable in the mountains. I had all my equipment. Before we left Toronto, Kees had delivered a brand new pair of Stöckli Vipers, the hottest skis with a snakeskin design on the surface. I saw them every day when I went out. All I had to do was put them on, when I was ready. My family didn't push me. They showed a lot of compassion. I was still having nightmares. I needed to do this on my own time.

On December 30, I caught the bus with them to the mountain. I brought my gear. I got on the chairlift with them, but at the top, I was frozen with fear. Brian lifted me off and encouraged me to keep going. "You can do this Carol, come with us, you'll be fine." I knew I wouldn't be fine and went home. Brian didn't force the issue, but a few days later, I tried again. I felt pretty good until I put my skis on and approached the chairlift. I didn't like the feel of the snow; I thought it was going to be tricky. I got more and more nervous going up the mountain with my family. On the hill, I was terrified of someone hitting me. I made one run and that was it. It wasn't even a run; I picked my way down the mountain as if I'd never been on skis before. While Brian, Hudson and Hilary kept on skiing, I went back to the hotel, shaking, feeling awful. The tremors were doing a wild dance. My neck and shoulders were so sore I had to spend a couple of hours icing them, using a hotel garment bag filled with ice from the machine down the hall. There was no triumph, no celebration. I thought, Maybe I'll never ski again. Maybe it's too much. I felt like a bit of a failure—that old childhood conditioning. What, you didn't do it? Try again.

After dinner, Brian said he'd hired a guide to work with me. "He's very nice, he's an older man, he's experienced, and he'll just ski with you until you feel comfortable." The next day, I met him. He was a charming Frenchman who'd been working at Chamonix for over 40 years. His daughter was about my age, he said, and she'd gone to Stanford University and become a lawyer and lived in California. He was very proud of her. I felt comfortable with him. He spoke four or five languages and he was easy going. We didn't talk about the accident or the injuries or why I needed a guide. I didn't have to explain myself.

I went up the chairlift with him, still feeling nervous, afraid of falling, afraid of losing my balance. I was a 48-year-old woman who was learning to ski again, after a lifetime of being fearless. He was unruffled by my behaviour. He led me down an easy run and somehow I followed him. He wasn't a great skier and he took his time. We just kept going up and chatting and coming down. I skied with him for four hours that first day. I was still awkward and hesitant on the runs but I went home with a sense of accomplishment. By the end of the second day with him, I was skiing faster than he was and feeling good on my skis. He kept choosing slower runs and I wanted faster runs. I'd be waiting for him at the bottom, eager to go up again. With icing at night for my muscles and gentle skiing during the day, I was gaining confidence and having fun on the slopes. I wasn't about to go out of bounds or jump off a cornice, but I could handle the basic stuff, up and down. It never occurred to me that I'd go off piste again. I didn't think about it and didn't feel I was missing much. After a few days, I thanked the guide and started skiing by myself. Then Brian and Hudson took off for the backcountry and reported on the great time they were having, while Hilary and I skied together. We had so much fun. Then I took a day off, and took it easy. Never done that before in the Alps. A new me was emerging, a more laid back, more relaxed person. I didn't have to push so hard.

In the second week of January, Hudson flew back to Nortre Dame and the three of us moved on to Courmayeur, where Hilary was enrolled in school. A beautiful village in Italy, high up in the Alps, Courmayeur is on the backside of Mont Blanc, or, as the Italians refer to it, Monte Bianco. We had rented a two-bedroom flat in a new, four-storey apartment chalet. It promised a spectacular view of the Alps from the balcony and it delivered. I was thrilled by our living quarters and the prospect of staying there for eight weeks. I walked Hilary to school in the morning while Brian headed out for a day of backcountry skiing. I wasn't ready to go with him. I was slowing down and finding it pleasurable to have time to think and reflect. I saw myself standing in my family doctor's office a month earlier, showing her my tremor. I remembered her question: "Have you ever considered writing about the accident. In Courmayeur, her idea flooded into me and I thought, Yes, I'll try to write about it. I went to a stationery store and bought a thick, lined pad of paper. After a pleasant morning of skiing in bounds, I sat down to write. When it was time to pick up Hilary from school that afternoon, I was astonished at how time had flown by. The words flew out of me, 20,000 words in two days.

There was no rushing, no traffic, nothing to take my mind off getting healthy, exercising, icing the painful parts and trying to figure out what had happened to me and write it down. It was a calming environment and a wonderful place to heal. I was able to recognize my good fortune. I had survived the accident and was now able to be in the Alps with my family. I was filled with gratitude toward all the people who'd helped me. I still hadn't talked much about what I was feeling but Brian, through his actions demonstrated his devotion in ways that were incredibly meaningful. I'd felt alone on the mountain, but during rehab I was fully supported. And as I wrote, he read, and he learned. We both did. Until I put pen to paper, I hadn't let myself look at what had happened.

The accident had shattered the sense of security I'd had in the world, just as my father's death had done. The trauma made me endlessly fearful. Now the circle was knitting together and I was beginning to feel whole again. The healing came from rehab, from my own hard work, from my family, from my childhood in Northern Ontario and the powerful survival instinct I carried with me. When I was in a traumatic state, all I had was my family. I hung on to them tight. Everything else seemed insignificant. All I cared about was getting better so I could participate in life with them. They gave me the strength to survive because of the joy they brought me.

While we were in Courmayeur, Brian had to go back to Canada for six days to tie up some business dealings, and when he returned, he brought my laptop computer so I could work on my story. I couldn't type for long without my neck aching but printing out my words on paper, on hard copy, felt good. The nightmares ended in the Italian Alps. I no longer played the tapes of endless falling in my head at night. And my physical challenges were also over, I thought.

Back in Canada, I resumed running my household and Brian returned to work. I would sit at my computer and try to do simple things, like exchanging emails, and realized I couldn't yet contemplate going back to work. My neck and back were too sore. I had limitations I had to accept. Visa Canada called and inquired about my availability but I had to say no, not at the moment. Even so, most of my day was not consumed with rehab. I was able to do more with Hilary; we'd go grocery shopping and she'd do her trademark "knock" on melons to find the one that was perfectly ripe. She always got it right. I watched her play sports and helped with her homework. I made blueberry pies. Brian and I went to movies. My neck was still quite jammed and I couldn't run but I was able to exercise. I still had tremors but I was in pretty good shape.

In September 2005 at my nephew Fraser's wedding rehearsal dinner, I was giving a toast to him and I started shaking. This was becoming a familiar pattern: whenever I got into a pressured situation, the tremors elevated. My hands shook so hard, jerking the piece of paper on which I'd written my speech, that Brian reached forward to steady me and held the paper firm. I was shocked and felt l had to say something to all the people watching me. I didn't want anyone to think I was drunk or had a bad case of MS or Parkinson's Disease.

"I've had a ski injury," I said, "and I have a tremor as a result." I went on with my speech, but I felt terribly vulnerable and exposed—almost naked in front of people, afraid of being subjected to their ridicule. To my great relief nothing terrible happened, and a man approached me after to share his own difficulties and recommend a cranial sacral therapist, whom I later tried (with middling results).

That fall, my friend Ursula Higgins, a physician who lives in my neighborhood, suggested Brian and I visit her and her husband Paul in February 2006 at their place in Vail, Colorado. This became a new goal for me. For months I trained for Vail and watched my tremors like a hawk. They acted up constantly. When we flew to Vail in February, a full year and a half after the accident, I took my skis and skates, figuring that if the skiing didn't work out, I could skate. As it turned out, I skied full days, from 8:30 am to 3 pm, and started doing longer runs in bounds, in beautiful powder. My confidence was up, my skill level was improving. One day I fell and my left shoulder dislocated again, which was a terrible shock, but it slid back into the socket on its own, and felt better than it had after Brian and Kees put it back in at Las Leñas.

A few days later, I said, "Let's go off piste." The four of us hiked up East Vail Chutes, a half-hour climb—Ursula and Paul had never been in the backcountry before—and skied down the other side. It was fairly tricky, challenging terrain but they loved it and there was no hesitation from me. I didn't have a tremor, my legs were strong, I felt the rush of skiing through virgin powder, the invigoration that comes with off piste skiing. "I'm back," I said to Brian. We were ecstatic. That evening we toasted my full return to the mountains. I was like a kid jumping up and down, Wow, did you see that? I wasn't even shaking. Brian was thrilled for me.

Back home in Toronto, the tremors resurfaced. During March break, skiing off piste at Whistler, our old stomping ground, the tremors were elevated. I tried ignoring it, skiing out of bounds, pushing it, but the fear of falling re-emerged and I continued trembling, inside and out. Again my left shoulder popped out—and went back in, with more pain this time. But the snow conditions were so terrific, and Hilary was enjoying the backcountry terrain so much, at the age of 11, that I kept skiing. I was thrilled to see her having so much fun. Ever since my accident, Hilary had become extremely cautious about skiing on steep runs she considered at all dangerous. "I'm a scaredy cat," she told Brian and I. We always respected her decisions when she said, "No, I'm not going down that," and never tried to push her. In fact, Brian encouraged me "to be more like Hilary," and set tighter limits for myself. I noticed that Brian was happy to ski with Hilary on "easier" runs, and they spent more time together biking and playing golf and hockey and tennis.

The accident changed him, too.

Gradually, I got better. My fractured ribs, back, neck and left shoulder healed. My left rib cage felt almost normal, my left shoulder was very strong—despite the two dislocations since the accident—and the feeling returned in my left side. I could breathe without pain and eventually got full feeling back in my left arm, too.

The relief I felt—that I wasn't going to be permanently disabled—was followed by the awareness of how much suffering there is in the world, so much worse than my own. I realized how incredibly lucky I was to be alive. I tried to minimize my anger—anger at myself for "being so stupid" on the mountain, for risking my life when I had two children to look after, for struggling through a long, slow recovery process that didn't go as fast as I wanted it to. The frustration waned as I became more accepting and tolerant of my own pain, and worked so hard to get better. Gradually, I accepted the changes that had to take place in my day-to-day life. Brian told me to focus on the positive. "You've got the freedom and resources to get better on your own time schedule," he said. It was true. I was grateful for all the hard work we'd both done in the years leading up to the accident, enabling me to buy time, to not have to work, to get well.

Looking back, my approach to recovery was fairly straightforward. I wanted to own the accident and not put the blame on anybody else. I was responsible for my own actions. I made the decision to jump off that ridge and go down that chute. If you want to get well, you can't go through life blaming other people. That I know for sure.

I armed myself with as much knowledge as I could about my condition and normal expectations for healing. I realized

I had to feel the pain. If I was on so many painkillers I didn't even know the extent of my injuries, how could I get better? I had to inhabit my own body and get over the fear of my pain. I didn't make friends with it but I learned to tolerate it. Even now, writing this book, two years after the accident, I can wake up in pain. But I've learned to be patient with it. And accept the suffering.

I shifted my perspective, recognizing that I was on a long journey. Rather than fighting the process—I've got to change doctors, find a better physiotherapist, search out a magical cure—I gradually accepted my limitations, adjusted my daily routines, asked for and accepted support. This was a big one for me. I let down my guard and showed "weakness," and it was okay. I was able to be grateful for what I could do. Acceptance—I am where I am—is important for recovery.

As is the determination to set goals and work toward them—which gave me a sense of progress over time, even if it was at a snail's pace. I made a pact with myself: I would never give up, even though some days I felt defeated. I would get up the next day, ready to try again. All I had was my own effort, and I embraced it. I made daily commitments, no matter how small. Three hours a day, every day, doing one-inch head nods.

It's a waste of time to think, Why me? Everyone suffers. Everyone makes mistakes. I paid attention to the big picture. I cared for and showed compassion to others. That's what got me out of myself and gave me a sense of humility and connection.

I was feeling better. I could continue to be a loving wife and mother, and I would make a decision about returning to work as I got stronger—but I was in no rush. The early goals of my career seemed so distant. I'd been driven to compete, to jump through corporate hoops, to rise to the top. Now I was readjusting my values. In the blink of an eye I'd lost my balance on top of a treacherous mountain and fallen 2,000 feet. I'd almost died. The strength I'd gained from my struggle to recover gave new meaning to my life, to my love for my family.

Life is impermanent. Death comes when it will; we have no control over it. My father's death changed me permanently, as did my accident. I survived a catastrophe, I experienced a profound sense of gratitude at being given a second chance at life. I thought the terror was behind me.

Then I went walking with a friend in the Rosedale ravine, two years after the accident, and I fell. My tremors returned, and I experienced emotions so overwhelming that I had to seek the help of a trauma therapist. Once again, I got the message: you don't know what you don't know. I had dealt with most of my physical problems, I thought. Now came the hard part: the emotional and mental anguish. I would have to learn compassion for myself.

"Post-traumatic stress disorder (PTSD) is an anxiety disorder that can develop after exposure to a terrifying event or ordeal in which grave physical harm occurred or was threatened….Among those who may experience PTSD are military troops who served in the Vietnam and Gulf Wars; rescue workers involved in the aftermath of disasters like the terrorist attacks on New York City; survivors of accidents, rape, physical and sexual abuse and other crimes; immigrants fleeing violence in their countries….Many people with PTSD repeatedly re-experience the ordeal in the form of flashback episodes, memories, nightmares or frightening thoughts, especially when they are exposed to

events or objects reminiscent of the trauma. Anniversaries of the event can also trigger symptoms. People with PTSD also experience emotional numbness and sleep disturbances, depression, anxiety and irritability or outbursts of anger. Feelings of intense guilt are also common." From the U.S. National Institute of Mental Health.

CHAPTER NINE

From Nightmares to Dreams

ON MONDAY, MAY 22, 2006, two years after the accident, I was in bed, reading a few short pages—the brief description of the accident that begins this book. Though it was a pleasant spring evening, I was suddenly very cold and started to shake. My body went numb. I pulled up the duvet to try to get warm and turned out the light. I closed my eyes but sleep would not come. The room was moving. I felt myself falling and falling and falling into the couloir. The nightmare was back, for the first time in a long time. I was shocked to find myself terrorized. Everything was whirling and swirling, unstoppable. The original nightmares had been mostly black and white; these were vivid and colourful and much more frightening. My mind was going crazy. Brian was out of town, Hudson was at Notre Dame, Hilary was asleep, and I was alone with my demons. What was happening? What was wrong with me?

After virtually no sleep, I got up the next morning, my nightgown soaked with sweat. I made breakfast for Hilary and tried to carry on as usual, pretending I was all right. I drove her to school. My tremors were elevated. Hoping to relax, I went walking in the Rosedale ravine with a close friend. Still shaken from the night before, I didn't tell her what I was feeling. I wasn't a whiner. And what would l have said? That I thought I was losing my mind?

As I walked across a log over a mud puddle, I fell backwards off the log, and landed with all my weight on my left shoulder. Suddenly I was back in Las Leñas after the crash, and the experience wasn't just scary, it was vicious, it gripped me with total intensity, with no mercy. I was crying and screaming and shaking—symptoms I hadn't even displayed after the accident. My friend said the look in my eyes was one of "pure terror." She helped me up and got me home. I assured her I'd be okay and told her she didn't have to stay. I didn't want her to see how "crazy" I felt.

I sat and shook and couldn't function. Nothing like this had ever happened to me before. If I'd been told that people experienced flashbacks so real they felt thrown back into the traumatic event, I would have said, *People imagine things*. But this was no figment of my imagination. I didn't understand that the trauma was still alive in my mind, and my mind had more influence over my body than I knew.

I called my family doctor. She said I was having flashbacks and wrote a new prescription, originally provided by a neurologist, for anti-anxiety medication. I got the pills and took them. I went to see the physiotherapist, to try to find some relief for my back and arm. But the pills didn't work and the terror didn't diminish. Later that same evening, trying to calm myself down, I went out for a walk with the dog. Our street is flat, with no sudden bumps or crevasses, but somehow I ended up falling backwards onto the sidewalk. I cried out in front of a neighbour who was passing by. He helped me up. "Oh, it's just a little problem with my balance," I said, embarrassed. Did he think I was drunk?

I retreated into the house. All the old feelings from the accident flooded back—the fear of dying, the overwhelming terror, the endless sensation of falling. This disability—if that's what this was—quickly robbed me of self-confidence. I felt so vulnerable and spaced out. How could I even leave my house if I was not able to control my movements? How could I look after Hilary? That night, and for many nights to come, Brian took over. I wouldn't have made it without his support. Any marriage would have been tested to its limits, but Brian was always steady and never gave up.

The next morning, the day of my birthday, I thought, that's it, I can't do it, I have to cancel the book. Only a week after signing on with my publisher and starting to work on the manuscript, I sent an email to Judy Steed, the writer I was collaborating with.

From: Carol Grant Sullivan
Sent: Wednesday, May 24, 2006 8:31 AM
To: Judy Steed
Subject: Carol's book

Dear Judy,
Good morning, it's my birthday today and therefore it is supposed to be a great day for me. Instead it feels like

I am in the centre of a nightmare. Since receiving and reading the Prologue on Monday night, I have been thrown back into the terror of falling in the couloir and I can't seem to get any relief. I took an unexpected and ghastly fall yesterday in the Rosedale Ravine while walking with a friend and again, last night before bed, I took another tumble onto my back, while walking on my street. Both falls came out of nowhere and in both cases I was falling backwards in slow motion as I did in the Andes. I am not sleeping and my tremor is elevated to levels of a year and a half ago.

I tried working on and off yesterday, talking to Brian and Kees, checking facts and events for the book, but I can't read the details about the accident in the Prologue. I can't even look at the piece.

I hate being like this but I feel I must put the project on hold for now. Give me a couple of days to see if I can sort this out. I will call.

Carol

I talked to Judy on the phone. I told her I couldn't go forward. I was not psychologically able to revisit the accident. I cried all day. I was falling apart. Was the rest of my life going to be like this? How was I going to put myself back together again? How would my family cope? I felt defeated. Was all the progress I'd made just an illusion? How could I have gone back to skiing the steeps in the backcountry this past winter and still be suffering such horrifying feelings of terror?

Within a few days, things began to turn around. The longer I sat, the more I realized I had to write this book. If I walked away from it, I'd be trapped in this cycle for the rest of my life. I'd be a victim forever, hiding from the accident, unable to face reality. Brian was incredibly encouraging. "You need to do this book, Carol," he said. "You can do it." And he told me something I didn't know. "The day after your accident," he said, "I skied to the base of that goddam mountain, by myself, and yelled and screamed and swore at it like a crazy man. I hope nobody heard me. I think I probably sounded insane." I don't know why, but that cheered me up. The thought occurred to me later that maybe he'd been trying to protect me from his own pain.

I resumed working on the book with Judy Steed, but she was reluctant to talk about the accident with me until I went to see a trauma therapist. My first visit to Mary Armstrong, a psychotherapist who specializes in trauma, was enlightening. I was feeling a little nervous when I walked into her office; As soon as we started to talk, I began to shake. Mary noticed the sudden, elevated tremors in my legs. I told her that I thought the tremors were a physiological problem, caused by nerve damage—though my doctors had assured me I had no significant neurological problems. I had chosen not to believe them and was working on the assumption that I still had nerve damage to repair.

As my tremors kicked in, in front of Mary, I said, "The tremors are always in my body. Sometimes they diminish to a low level and aren't visible, and at other times, like now, they're very elevated." We discussed the fact that the trauma was alive in me, and Mary said it was normal that my body was reacting as it was. I wasn't crazy. I knew I had recovered physically from the accident with the intensive physical rehab I had carried out, yet it never occurred to me that my body was shaking due to the psychological damage from the trauma of the accident.

Mary said that the shaking could be my body's way of attempting to rid itself of the trauma. I realized I had been hiding this from everyone (even from myself) for so long that I had accepted the tremors as something I would simply have to live with for the rest of my life. Mary's explanation of the force of post-traumatic stress and her idea that these tremors of mine were absolutely part of my body's way of dealing with the trauma was a major discovery. The light bulb went on. I had repaired physically but needed desperately to repair psychologically before I could be whole again.

Having felt trapped in a life of fear and terror that no one could understand, I was relieved to be able to talk to someone who knew what I was going through. Mary explained the symptoms of post-traumatic stress disorder and suggested a very clear method of treatment. There was a definition for what I was experiencing. That helped. As did the awareness that— just as Sue Deacon, my physiotherapist, had the skills to guide me through physical rehabilitation—Mary could help me deal with the emotional and psychological effects of trauma. Once I understood I had new things to learn, I felt much better. There was a path out of this overwhelming bombardment of flashbacks. I became an eager student again.

Over the next few months, as we worked together, Mary suggested I put the book on hold for a while because the accident was still so alive in me. But I couldn't. I had to push through. It was my nature. She said that the memory of the accident needed to be reprocessed and stored in a part of my brain where it could be integrated and not cause me so much fresh pain, as if it had happened yesterday. One of her treatment techniques was EMDR, which stands for Eye

Movement De-sensitization and Reprocessing, which was used to treat survivors of the September 11, 2001 terrorist attacks on the World Trade Center in New York. The process was simple: We would sit facing each other. I would close my eyes and visualize an aspect of the accident, hold the image in my mind, and then open my eyes and watch the light on the tip of a wand as Mary moved the wand back and forth in front of me.

After EMDR sessions, I felt calm, centred and grounded. And sometimes exhausted. Gradually, over time, my tremors diminished and the memory of the accident seemed to settle into a place that was more manageable. Mary also taught me techniques to avoid flashbacks and deal with painful emotions. I was in a psychological healing period, she explained, and until I healed, I would not have normal coping strengths.

I realized I had been—and still was—hyper-alert, hyper-vigilant and preoccupied with danger, which made it hard for me to concentrate on the present. As I'd healed physically and emerged from the cocoon of numbness, I had so much on my mind that had been hidden, that couldn't be spoken, I frequently lost my train of thought. I'd be talking to Hilary or Brian and hesitate, mid-sentence, forgetting what I intended to say. "Finish your sentence, Mom," Hilary would chide. My memory seemed vague, my handwriting weak and scrawling. I was easily thrown off, couldn't cope with stress, and had a hard time making decisions. Put me in a car in traffic and I'd be sweating, under pressure to decide whether to turn left or right. It was all too much. I had been faking normal behaviour for so long that I couldn't keep it up anymore. The pose of a stiff upper lip and overall mental toughness was no longer available to me. To top it all off, I was still riddled with guilt about the accident, for being so stupid to have risked my life trying to ski down a dangerous mountain.

Mary Armstrong: When Carol first came to see me, she said, 'This is ridiculous, I survived the accident, I got out of there, I'm fine—but I can't get on with my life.' She thought she was going crazy, but what she was experiencing made sense in the context of trauma.

In a traumatized state, people can have a constant feeling of being unsafe, of being threatened, and these feelings can be pervasive even though, as in Carol's case, her accident happened two years ago. Dr. Robert Scaer, an American neurologist with long experience treating the pain resulting from accidents, calls it "the survival brain." In his book, The Body Bears the Burden: Trauma, Dissociation, and Disease, *he writes that survivors of intolerable, inescapable events are unable to relegate these memories to the past.*

Carol's first trauma was the fall off the mountain. Her second trauma was getting up on her feet and skiing out of that valley, driven by the fear of frostbite and amputation. She thought her numb shoulder and arm were frostbitten; she thought she would lose them. Now, when she gets cold or stressed, she shivers and shakes and the tremor is elevated. Perhaps her body is remembering the sensation of numbness, of freezing, the threat of amputation.

The memories of trauma are stored in the right hemisphere of the brain—the emotional brain—and lower down, in the primitive or mammalian brain. It's as if the emotional brain gets frozen in the past. When we do

EMDR, we sit facing each other, therapist and client. She concentrates on an image that evokes the upsetting feeling. I move the light wand back and forth while her eyes follow the light from left to right, from left brain to right brain over and over again, providing bi-lateral stimulation, enabling the traumatized right brain to gain access to the rationality of the left brain. If feelings become too intense or overwhelming, we take a break, come out of the trauma, and then dip in again. We don't want to revivify the trauma or re-traumatize the survivor. It's a careful process of finding a safe place, helping Carol find gentle ways to integrate the memory.

In my office, she is learning to stay in the present and deal with something awful that happened in the past. And she's doing very well being compassionate with herself, which was hard for her, at first."

Gradually, I began to see things differently. I had never considered counselling or therapy before, so it was all new to me—the feeling that Mary was walking beside me as I gained insight into myself, helping me explore this stage of my journey. The guideposts she gave me were deceptively simple: Accept my feelings. Be with myself in the moment. Be compassionate with myself.

It might sound easy, but compassion for myself came slowly. It was HARD. I'd been raised to think of others first. When Mary talked to me about caring for myself, being gentle with myself, I recoiled. Growing up with competitive older brothers, and as an adult pursuing a high altitude sport dominated by men, I had absorbed a culture that exalted toughness and denigrated "wimps." In truth, you had to be tough to do extreme skiing. Yet at the same time, I was a woman. I had to learn the difference between narcissism—a level of absorption that's utterly selfish—and healthy self-care. It's something that can be difficult for women, especially when we've been socialized to put our families' needs first. But I'm learning. Mary says I can't afford more flashbacks like the ones I had after I first read the Prologue and fell in the ravine the next day—they're too damaging. So I work hard to not get over-stressed. I consciously consider situations that will and won't be good for me. I think about what it takes to keep me safe and warm and comfortable. I try to plan my day, and my life, at a comfortable pace; I don't always succeed, but I'm aware of the toll too much pressure takes. I avoid people who are negative or put me in tense situations. I protect myself. I say no to things that could harm me, events that are too stressful. I accept my present fragility. I am surprised it took me so long to wake up to my biggest injury of all... the psychological trauma.

It's a gift—the insight I've gained. Through the process of writing this book I have discovered the hidden power of trauma and my ability to overcome it. I'm a different woman today. The old Carol is gone. I was afraid to give her up, but I had no choice, it was imposed on me by trauma. I am beginning to embrace the new me, a more reflective, more inner-directed person. This is an ongoing process.

During my treatment with Mary Armstrong I learned to acknowledge the fragile, traumatic state I was in. This was very difficult for me, and for months after I first saw Mary, I would still find myself almost scoffing at the concept of trauma—the way the young off piste hotshots would. It's a long climb down from a self-image of physical strength and skill to accepting my limitations, to stop hiding them. To be who I am, now.

Mary helped me listen to my body and be gentle with myself. I stopped denying the emotional pain, the fear, guilt, sadness and terror. I lowered my expectations for physical conditioning and refocused energy on the psychological healing. I was incredibly grateful for her help, and learned at a deeper level how important it is to seek out experts and accept their guidance. Mary, who is also a yoga teacher, encouraged me to do yoga every day at home; the practice helped to focus my mind and relax my muscles. On calm days, I took uninterrupted, quiet time to think and pay attention to myself and open my mind to new possibilities, new ways of being, getting familiar with this strange new Carol who did yoga and acknowledged her feelings and didn't push herself to peak physical performance. I negotiated with myself to add activities that I thought would provide comfort. I concentrated on positive emotional experiences—happiness, joy, sharing, love, giving, having beautiful things around me to look at. Staying open to life.

Returning to the North, I slept in, one July morning at the cottage. Brian got up early and rigged the sailboat. He came back and woke me up, made me a cup of coffee, and said, "It's a beautiful day. Do you feel like going sailing?" I sailed out into the bay in the Laser, the blue and purple sail filling with wind, and he was on his windsurfer with its red sail. We tacked back and forth, crossing paths, racing across the lake.

I think of life "Before the Accident," and "After the Accident." Before, I was on automatic pilot, pushing forward no matter what. I didn't know how to back down. In our strength is our weakness. It was my drive, my never-say-die attitude that got me into trouble on the mountain, and ultimately saved my life.

As Mary helped me tell "the real story," I learned not to shy away from it and realized that gradually, I was separating myself from the trauma. That was then, this is now. Eventually the story will become a distant memory.

Today, I'm learning to respect my needs, to rebalance my life. My tremors are far less evident and when they surface they're a gentle reminder of the accident and the boundaries I have set around myself regarding danger, physical and emotional. I listen to my body; I have to. It starts pumping adrenalin when I feel stressed or at risk and it doesn't stop until the stress is eased.

As I reach the end of this book, I know I don't have all the answers. I feel passionate about raising awareness about the profound impact of trauma on people's lives—and how little most of us know about it. Counselling for victims of post-traumatic stress disorder is critically important. I know how desperately lost and frightened I was, and how treatment helped transform my life. If my story can give one person hope, I will be satisfied.

This life-balance journey will continue until the day I die. Change is constant. Life is impermanent. I was driven to compete from a very young age, and was burdened by a sense of "letting people down" and "not delivering" if I didn't do well. As I readjust my values, I see things differently. I am more accepting. I am finding ways to use my time wisely. To practice calmness of mind.

I have worked hard all my life to be a positive role model for my children and my friends, to contribute to my community. This all came easily to me. I skied hard because it gave me a thrill and a challenge like nothing else. I felt my best in the mountains. But my perspective has shifted. Nowadays, I can enjoy the simplicity of life, watching the birds outside the window, in the garden; the small pleasures I would have been too busy for, before the accident, now bring me joy. I look forward to returning to work, taking flight in new directions, open to new horizons.

The fear, self-doubt and guilt that troubled me with such intensity after the accident is fading and giving way to a new self-awareness that feels softer and more forgiving. The sense of urgency is gone. All that remains from the trauma I suffered is a distant memory of the accident. My tremors, if they surface, are a reminder of my good fortune. I am alive! I can watch my children mature. I can return to the mountains with Brian when I choose. My love affair with my husband continues and deepens.

Occasionally, I have a dream at night. If I fall, I always land in soft snow.

Laying down fresh tracks upon my return to the backcountry, *2006*

Glossary of Terms

Avalanche: *falling masses of snow that can contain rocks, trees, soil, or ice. An avalanche slide can cause death; skiers can be asphyxiated if buried or trapped under falling debris and dragged over rocks and cliff bands and into trees.*

Avalanche beacon: *body finder (also called a rescue transceiver) electronic device that emits a beeping signal when transmitting. Used in search and rescue, it shows the distance and direction to buried victims. Anyone going into an unpatrolled area of the mountains should wear an avalanche beacon strapped tightly to the top of the inside layer of clothing.*

Backcountry: *unprotected, unpatrolled, unmaintained area of mountains that generally attracts a limited number of skiers who are after extreme or exceptional skiing terrain and snow conditions. A key element of the backcountry is increased hazards and higher risks of unstable snow conditions because of sheer size and location of the terrain.*

Bluebird day: *combination of blue skies, clear weather and ideal snow conditions.*

Boilerplate: *very hard packed, sheer, icy snow that is normally caused by the sun heating it up and temperatures dropping to create an extremely hazardous condition. On steep terrain this type of snow is difficult to navigate over.*

Chute: *usually a long narrow access point that can be steep and difficult to ski, often leading to a wider slope down below.*

Cold smoke: *light powder snow that explodes into the air in skiers' faces as they descend the mountain.*

Cornice: *overhanging mass or lip of heavy snow usually formed at the top of a steep slope as a result of heavy winds. These formations can range in size from a curb to a house and can collapse or release under you, triggering a slide.*

Couloir: *steep, wide gully on the mountain side often where the best powder and high speed skiing is found because it is generally untreed and wide open.*

Crevasse: *deep fissure or crack in the snow or ice on a glacier; generally viewed as a dangerous obstacle or hazard to avoid.*

Chalet skiers: *humorous term used to describe less than enthusiastic skiers.*

Drop off: *steep entrance into a run usually involving jumping or leaping into an area to gain access to a slope.*

Extreme: *remote, severe, excessively dangerous conditions, going to great lengths to experience the ultimate.*

Fall Line: *most direct route from top to bottom of a mountain, usually refers to straight down—the way a pebble would fall if dropped from the summit of the mountain.*

Fracture Line: *line between weak and strong snow, crack in the snow often the clue that defines the crown or starting zone of an avalanche.*

Fresh tracks: *new ski turns in powder snow on mountain terrain previously not skied.*

Face of the mountain: *front of the mountain normally exposed to wind and weather elements including sun.*

Face shots: *powder snow hitting the face of a skier during descent.*

Hard core skier: *bold, strong, tough and dedicated skier able to resist or overcome difficult mountain conditions.*

Line: *route or path down the mountain.*

Licensed mountain guide: *a working professional, trained, certified and able to provide a high level of leadership in the mountains.*

Off-piste: *out of bounds, outside the resort boundary, unpatrolled area of the mountain, outside the ropes that indicate a patrolled mountain ski area.*

Open it up: *speeding up, letting your skis run without restrictions, accelerating.*

Poma: *a traditional surface lift attached to a cable transporting one person at a time up the side of a slope, often used on very steep terrain. Named after its manufacturer.*

Powder snow: *masses of dry, fine, light snow particles*

Probe: *collapsible pole used to pinpoint a buried body after you have tracked it down with a beacon, following an avalanche.*

Rip an edge: *carve a turn into the snow at high speed, on a steep angle.*

Skins/ Skinning up: *a velcro-like outside covering attached to the base of the ski for the purpose of resisting skidding backwards when attempting to climb a slope/ the process of walking up a mountain slope or ascending the slope with skis on.*

Steeps: *exaggerated, or sharpest slope of the mountain often most attractive to extreme skiers.*

Summit: *highest point, apex of the mountain that skiers /mountaineers aim for when undertaking a climb.*

Surface slide: *loose snow sliding in a single area moving down the slope in a triangular path, usually involving a light amount of snow and not capable of forming a dangerous avalanche.*

Virgin snow: *highest quality of snow, new snow that has yet to be touched by skiers, untracked.*

Vertical: *measurement of distance skied on each run or for the overall day. Also refers to height of drop off from horizontal position i.e. A 90 degree vertical drop.*

Carol in Zermatt, Switzerland, *2005*

Carol Grant Sullivan

Carol Grant Sullivan is an independent marketing consultant conducting business in the Canadian financial services sector. She has over 20 years of credit card experience including VISA, Canadian Financial Institutions, and American Express. Carol is also a private equity investor in real estate and consumer packaged goods.

Born into a prosperous Northern Ontario family and following her graduation from the University of Western Ontario, Carol first settled in the Canadian Rockies. Fascinated with mountaineering and backcountry skiing, she became an avid extreme skier, eventually dividing her time between the best off-piste slopes around the world and her family and business in Toronto. Carol has skied some of the most secluded and challenging terrain. Her backcountry experience encompasses the Andes, Alps, Dolomites, BC Coastals, Bugaboos, Caribous, Monashees, Selkirks, Tetons, and the Canadian & US Rockies.

Carol is the quintessential modern woman. She is the wife of a corporate executive, mother of two children, dedicated volunteer, elite athelete, and independent businesswoman.